FRESH MAINE SALADS

FRESH MAINE SALADS

Innovative Recipes from Appetizers to Desserts

Cynthia Finnemore Simonds

Photographs by Randall Smith

Drawings by the Author

Down East Books

ISBN: 0-89272-700-4   (13-digit) 978-082972-700-1

Design by Chilton Creative
Printed in China   (RPS)

5   4   3   2   1

Library of Congress Cataloging-in-Publication Data
Simonds, Cynthia Finnemore, 1966–
Fresh Maine salads : innovative recipes from appetizers to desserts /
Cynthia Finnemore Simonds ; photographs by Randall Smith.– 1st ed.
p. cm.
Includes index.
ISBN 0-89272-700-4 (trade pbk.)
1. Salads. I. Title.
TX740.S4694 2006
641.8'3–dc22
2005026001

Down East Books
A division of Down East Enterprise, Inc.
Publisher of *Down East*, the Magazine of Maine

Book orders: 1-800-685-7962
www.downeastbooks.com

CONTENTS

Introduction

9

Side Salads

13

Appetizer and Brunch Salads

27

Contents

Spreads to Complement Your Salads
41

Dinner Salads
45

Dessert Salads
61

Contents

Dressings and Marinades
67

Enhancements—The "Wow" Factor
81

Appendixes
95

Index
104

This book is dedicated with love
to Travis and Elizabeth—may their
taste buds keep growing.

INTRODUCTION

Compulsions of a "Foodie"

When I was twelve years old I decided to write a cookbook. That was in 1979. Thanks to years of running my own catering business, entertaining friends, and raising two wonderful children, I have put together a collection of recipes that allows me to realize that dream.

Many of us "foodies" can remember cooking when we were very young, and I am no exception. Luckily for me, my mom always said yes when I offered to help in the kitchen, and by the age of four I was reading recipes and baking my own cakes. I began catering for neighbors when I was thirteen, starting with intimate dinners, then branching out to ever larger parties. I remember catering one baby shower for 150 guests from a six-by-eight-foot kitchen that also housed the bar! (Eventually, that catering business would help put me through college.)

I'd use any excuse to get into the kitchen. When I had school assignments, especially in History, I'd always try to make my report about a food-related topic. I'd learn about women's roles and the recipes, ingredients, and cooking implements of a particular era. I would make a meal, dress in period costume, and bring in antique or reproduction food-preparation tools from that time.

I also started seeking out and recording recipes from my family when I was very young. A high school friend once gave me a beautiful blank book, thinking that I would use it for keeping a journal. Not likely! Instead, it became my own personal cookbook. That first notebook has now been joined by several others. I have a recipe box too—an old oak library-card file—but my favorite recipes still reside in the books on the kitchen shelf.

Salads, Fresh and Local

Food nourishes us. It gives us energy—fuel for our bodies. Even more important for me, though, is the comfort and pleasure found in sharing a good meal with others. I do love that "Mmmm" sound that fills the room as people take their first bite of some scrumptious dish. When we use fresh ingredients and prepare them with love, it nourishes more than just our muscles. The many people who have enjoyed the recipes you will find in these pages have been open with their opinions and willing to continue tasting as long as I keep creating.

I chose salads as the topic for this first cookbook because I love to work with fresh ingredients. I so enjoy creating recipes that are bursting with flavor, fun to prepare, and a pleasure to look at. Salad is a basic, delicious, wonderful addition to any meal—and as some of the following brunch and dinner recipes show, it can even serve as the main course. I hope that the trend toward eating healthier foods such as salads will create a trickle-down effect for our children. I am convinced that kids who grow up eating varied, tasty, exciting salads will continue that eating pattern throughout their lives.

Another wonderful thing about salads is that they can showcase the best local ingredients from one's home area. Many people might not immediately think "salad" when they hear the phrase "Maine foods," but in these pages I will show just how compatible those two concepts are. Here in Maine we have an active, enthusiastic farmer's market network (guides available at the www.getrealmaine.com website). These open-air markets are the best places to find anything grown or produced here in Maine, from fresh vegetables to wild mushrooms, specialty cheeses, condiments, and organic meats and eggs. The Maine Department of Agriculture, Food, and Rural Resources also publishes two helpful booklets: *Finding Maine Farmer's Markets: A Guide to Maine's Farmer's Markets* and *Finding Maine Foods and Farms: A Guide to Maine's Farms and Food Companies.*

Traditionally, Maine is known for its potato farms, blueberry barrens, and orchards. Farms across the state offer the opportunity to pick your own berries and apples, including heirloom varieties nurtured by growers committed to preserving America's agricultural heritage. Of course, Maine is famous for its lobster and other seafood. Aquaculture farms raise trout and salmon. Local smokehouses produce golden smoked mussels, trout, cheeses, and other specialties. All of these delicious products are excellent additions to salads.

In the recipes that follow, I indulge in a little bit of local pride by specifying "Maine potatoes," or "Maine maple syrup," or "Maine smoked trout," etc. You can, of course, substitute equivalent ingredients if you do not happen to live in Maine, but I'd certainly encourage you to try the genuine Maine-made products first. Beginning on page 96 you'll find information on how to order the wonderful Maine-made specialty foods listed in my recipes.

Make These Recipes Your Own

One of my favorite things to do with cookbooks is to jot notes in them. When I make a recipe I write in the date, who I made it for or what occasion we celebrated, and what I did differently that time. Two of my favorite cookbooks are the *King Arthur Flour 25th Anniversary Cookbook* and the *McCalls Cookbook* (Random House, 1963). Their pages are stained and covered with notes. It always makes me smile when I look through them and remember meals past.

This is what I hope for you—that you use this book for yourself and for your family. Write in it. Make notes of what you like and how you would change things to fit your own taste. Add more or less of an ingredient if that's what tastes right for you. This is *your* book.

A Few Important Acknowledgments

I have loved to cook for as many years as I can remember. There are a few people who have helped me along the way.

I would like to thank my mom, Nancy Finnemore, for instilling in me a spirit of creativity in life and in the kitchen.

Thanks to my children, Travis and Elizabeth, for reminding me of the wonder in little things.

Thanks to my husband, Sherwood Olin, for his support, love, and kindness, and certainly, for his willingness to say "Sure" whenever I asked, "Would you taste this?"

A special thank-you goes out to the woman who helped me begin my career in the food business, Linda B. Wagner. Thank you for having faith in my culinary skills and helping me nurture them through the classics of cuisine.

My editor, Karin Womer, has proven to be a wonderful mentor and translator of what I really meant to say. Thank you, Karin, for helping my voice ring true.

—C.F.S.

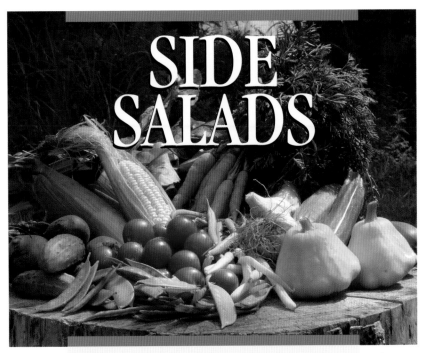

SIDE SALADS

E very day we should be eating at least five half-cup servings of vegetables. The following recipes provide several options for delicious and easy side dishes to enhance your meals.

Apple, Broccoli, and Dried Fruit Salad with Maple-Garlic Dressing

My friend Anne created a delicious salad with these ingredients, and developed a recipe that we can adapt in many different ways. This version is my favorite.
Serves 6 to 8

Salad:
- 2 large heads broccoli
- 1 c dried fruit (I particularly love dried cherries and apricots)
- 2 large Granny Smith apples
- 2 T fresh lemon juice
- ½ c sunflower seeds, pecans, or walnuts (optional)

Dressing:
- 1 c mayonnaise
- 2 cloves garlic, minced
- ¼ c pure Maine maple syrup
- ½ t salt
- a few grinds of pepper
- ⅛ t cayenne

Wash and cut the broccoli into bite-size pieces. Cut the dried fruit so all the pieces are about the size of large raisins. Wash and core the apples and cut them into ¾-inch chunks. Toss them in the lemon juice.

In a small bowl, whisk together the dressing ingredients.

In a large bowl, place the broccoli, dried fruit, apples, and seeds or nuts (if desired), and toss together. Pour the dressing over the salad and fold it together well, ensuring that everything is evenly coated and distributed. Chill for at least 30 minutes.

Serve with a sprinkle of sunflower seeds, if desired.

Zippy, Crunchy Summer Salad

This salad is a bit spicy, and is delicious alongside a bowl of chili or a plate of nachos. It has that south-of-the-border taste while still remaining crisp and cool. Adjust the spice elements to your taste.
Serves 8 to 10

Salad:
  2 medium tomatoes
  2 bunches of scallions (about 12)
  1 large red bell pepper
  1 large green bell pepper
  1 small head cabbage
  5 large carrots
  ½ c Vidalia onion, coarsely chopped
  16 oz can kidney beans
    (or Great Northern beans)

Dressing:
  ½ c red wine vinegar
  1 T cumin
  1 T fresh lemon juice
  1 lime, zested and juiced
  1 t sugar, honey, or Splenda sweetener
  1 t salt
  1 T oregano
  2 t white pepper
  2 t chili powder
  2 jalapeños, finely chopped
  ½ c fresh parsley, chopped fine
  ½ c fresh cilantro, chopped fine
  1 T shallots, finely chopped
  ½ c olive oil

Wash and coarsely chop the tomatoes. Wash and trim the scallions; slice thinly. Wash, seed, and chop the peppers into ¾" pieces. Wash and core the cabbage and slice into bite-size pieces. Peel and chop the carrots into ¾" pieces. Add the coarsely chopped Vidalia onion. Drain the kidney beans. Place all of the vegetables in a large bowl; toss and chill for 30 minutes.

In a small bowl, whisk together the vinegar, cumin, lemon and lime juice, sweetener (of your choice), salt, oregano, white pepper, and chili powder. Add the chopped jalapeños, parsley, cilantro, and shallots. Whisk in the olive oil.

Pour dressing over vegetables and toss well. Serve chilled.

Crisp Salad with Shallot Marinade

This salad is wonderful for the hot days of summer, since it contains no lettuce to wilt. The many green vegetables are cool and crunchy, and instead of a traditional dressing, this one boasts a "marinade." It is ideal for a buffet: The bite-size pieces are easily eaten with just a fork, and the fresh taste makes a wonderful accompaniment to any entrée.

The veggies can be chopped the day before, and the marinade tossed in on the morning of the day you'll serve it. It's best to let this salad marinate for at least an hour (but not overnight) before serving.

Serves 8 to 10 generously

Dressing:
  2 T fresh parsley, chopped
  1 T fresh oregano, chopped
    (or 1 t dried oregano)
  2 T garlic, minced
  4 T shallots, minced
  ½ c wine or white vinegar
  2 T sugar (or Splenda sweetener)
  ½ t salt
  ½ t fresh cracked black pepper
  6 to 8 oz extra virgin olive oil

Salad:
  2 bunches of celery
  4 medium cucumbers
  1 napa or Chinese cabbage
  1 bok choy cabbage
  4 leeks
  1 bunch fresh parsley
  1 box sprouts (of your choice)
  1 head cauliflower
  1 bunch scallions

In a medium glass or stainless-steel bowl, place the parsley and oregano. Add the garlic, shallots, vinegar, sugar, salt, and pepper. Whisk together for one minute. Be sure all of the ingredients are well blended and the sugar is dissolved.

Slowly drizzle the oil into the bowl as you whisk. Continue whisking until all of the oil is incorporated. Store in an airtight container in the refrigerator until you are ready to serve.

Wash the vegetables carefully. Cut the ends off the celery; peel and seed the cukes. Cut the core out of the cabbages, separating the leaves and rinsing well.

Cut the root end off of each leek. Trim green leaves to within 2 inches of white section. Make a slit up and all the way through the white part of the leeks, and gently rinse them to be sure they are free of sand. Rinse the parsley. Wash the sprouts well, and drain.

Remove and discard any green leaves from the cauliflower, thoroughly washing all of the white florets.

Cut the root end off of each scallion, discarding any discolored layers. Slice the scallions into ¼-inch pieces, and cut all of the other vegetables into bite-size pieces (no larger than ¾ of an inch; remember, these pieces should fit easily into your mouth).

Place the clean, dry vegetables in a beautiful bowl. (If you are making this ahead of time, they can be refrigerated overnight in an airtight container or resealable plastic bags.)

Before serving, whisk or shake the dressing well, drizzling it over the salad. Toss well to ensure that all the vegetables are evenly coated. You can dress this salad hours before serving, as long as you keep it well chilled.

If you prefer to make a smaller amount of this salad, simply reserve half of the cabbages, cauliflower, and celery after chopping; they make a delightful stir-fry! Use the other half of the dressing as your stir-fry sauce.

Spicy Five-Bean Salad

This tangy salad is an ideal accompaniment for grilled chicken, sure to please your palate! Use precooked or canned black, navy, broad, or garbanzo beans. Edamame are often found in the frozen vegetables section at the gracery store.
Serves 6 to 8

Salad:
  2 c black beans
  2 c navy beans
  2 c garbanzo beans
  1 c broad beans
  2 c edamame (soybeans)
  1 bunch fresh parsley, washed and chopped
  4 scallions, washed and chopped

Dressing:
  1 c olive oil
  ¾ c red wine vinegar
  2 T cumin
  2 limes, zested and juiced

  1 T fresh lemon juice
  2 t sugar or Splenda sweetener
  1 T fresh oregano, chopped
  1 T chili powder
  1 T fresh parsley, chopped
  ¼ t Tabasco sauce (or more to your taste)
  2 t salt
  1 T white pepper

Toss all the beans together with parsley and scallions.

Whisk together all of the ingredients for the dressing. Pour over beans and toss until evenly coated.

Marinate the salad for at least an hour, or overnight.

Warm and Creamy Parmesan Spinach Salad

When you're in the mood for comfort food, this scrumptious dish is the perfect choice. Its creamy texture and rich flavor make it a delightful accompaniment for roast chicken or beef.
Serves 6 to 8

24 oz (two large bags) frozen spinach, defrosted
8 oz fresh baby spinach
8 oz cream cheese (you can use Neufchatel reduced-fat cheese, if you prefer)
1 small Vidalia onion, grated or chopped in a food processor
1 c Parmesan cheese, freshly grated
1½ t fresh ground black pepper
salt to taste
1 4-oz can sliced water chestnuts, drained
¼ c chopped fresh chives
¼ t cayenne pepper (optional)

Place the frozen spinach in a bowl and microwave to defrost. (If you prefer to use the stovetop, heat the spinach slowly in a medium saucepan until thawed.)

Wash the baby spinach and trim any long stems. Set aside.

Place cream cheese and onion in a medium saucepan over low heat. When the cream cheese melts, add Parmesan cheese and black pepper.

Drain the defrosted frozen spinach until dry, wringing it out if necessary. Stir spinach into the sauce, seasoning with a sprinkle of salt (to taste) and cayenne pepper (if desired). Let the mixture sit over the lowest heat possible for 10 minutes, stirring often.

When the mixture is warm and creamy, stir in the fresh baby spinach and water chestnuts.

Serve immediately with grilled chicken, on a bed of greens, or even as a topping for pasta. Garnish with the chopped chives.

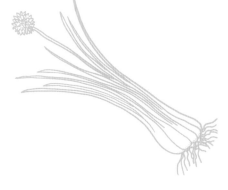

Caswell Church Supper Potato Salad

The highlight of a trip to Grammy Finnemore's farm was the Sunday church supper. Everyone in the little church would bring their favorite covered dish, and we would all share in the potluck. Grammy often made the potato salad. Even though we all have adaptations of a potato salad recipe from our childhood, this one has always proven to be a crowd-pleaser. Best made with fresh new potatoes as you can leave the skins on.
Serves 8 to 10 generously

Salad:
5 lbs Maine potatoes
a sprinkle of salt
2 cloves garlic, peeled
6 eggs, hard-boiled and peeled
1 c chopped celery

Dressing:
2 c mayonnaise
2 t celery salt or Beau Monde seasoning
20 chives, washed and minced
½ t salt
1 T sugar or Splenda sweetener
1 t pepper
2 T white vinegar

Wash the potatoes and cut into chunks. Place in a large saucepan and cover with water. Add a sprinkle of salt and two peeled cloves of garlic. Boil until fork-tender, about 15 minutes. Be sure to cook the potatoes until they are no longer crunchy in the center (but not mushy). Drain the potatoes and place in a large bowl. Chill for 30 minutes.

While the potatoes are cooking, you can also boil the eggs. Place them in a saucepan and cover with cool water. Bring the pot to a boil and simmer for 10 minutes. Turn off the heat and let them sit until the potatoes are done.

Rinse and peel the eggs and chop them coarsely into a small bowl. Cover and chill for 30 minutes.

In a medium bowl, stir together the dressing ingredients until well blended.

When the potatoes and eggs are chilled, add the chopped celery to the potatoes. Gently fold in the dressing. Add the chopped eggs and incorporate. Make sure there are no pockets of dry potatoes or dressing.

If you grow chives in your garden, the blossoms are a wonderful, spicy addition, both as an ingredient and a garnish.

If you make your salad ahead, wait until the last minute to dress it, as the potatoes will absorb the dressing if you mix it all in the day before. If it is too dry, you can add a bit more mayonnaise.

Sweet-and-Sour German Potato Salad

My mom used to make this warm and tangy salad, always delicious with grilled bratwurst or any kind of barbecue. Both sweet and salty, it holds its own alongside other flavorful foods, with plenty of delicious potato to soak up the wonderful dressing.
Serves 6 to 8

Salad:
  6 large Maine potatoes
  1 large Vidalia onion

Dressing:
  1 lb bacon, diced
  ¾ c yellow onion, finely chopped
  3 T flour
  ½ c white vinegar
  ¾ c water
  1 T celery seeds
  3 T sugar
  1½ t salt
  1 t fresh ground black pepper

Wash and trim the potatoes and Vidalia onion, peeling the potatoes if you like. Cut the potatoes and onion into quarters.

In a large saucepan, boil the potatoes and onion until the potatoes are fork-tender, but not mushy—about 15 minutes. Drain the water (reserving it if you are making foccacia, see p. 92). When the potatoes and onion are cool enough to handle, chop them into bite-size pieces.

In a large pan, fry bacon till crisp. Remove the bacon with a slotted spoon and drain on paper towel; crumble and set aside.

Add the ¾ c yellow onion to bacon fat in pan and cook 5 to 8 minutes, till onion is soft. With a slotted spoon, remove onion and set aside with the bacon.

Whisk flour into bacon fat. Add the vinegar, water, celery seeds, sugar, salt, and pepper. Heat to a boil; then, set pan on medium heat and cook till thickened.

Add potatoes, cooked Vidalia onion, bacon, and sautéed yellow onion. Gently stir to coat the potatoes.

Serve while warm.

Dilled New Potato Salad

Unlike traditional Maine potato salad, this one is lighter and flavored with fresh dill and lemon, giving it a delightful taste. Try it using low-fat ingredients if you like. It is especially beautiful garnished with pansies or nasturtiums (the latter adding a peppery flavor that enhances the lemon and dill).
Serves 4 to 6 generously

Salad:

2 lbs very small new Maine potatoes
2 baby Vidalia onions
1 c grated carrots
2 hard-boiled eggs, peeled and chopped

Dressing:

⅔ c sour cream
1 c mayonnaise
3 T fresh dill, chopped
3 T fresh parsley, chopped
¼ c fresh lemon juice
2 t lemon zest, minced
½ t salt
½ t white pepper

Wash the potatoes well and cook in salted boiling water until just tender (but not mushy). Chunk them into bite-size pieces (leaving the skins on) and place in a large bowl. Slice the baby Vidalia onions thinly and toss with the potatoes. Add the carrots and chopped, hard-boiled eggs, gently tossing all ingredients together.

In a small bowl, whisk together the dressing ingredients. Pour over vegetables and toss gently to coat, being careful not to crush the potatoes.

Garnish with colorful and edible flowers.

Mushroom and Caramelized Onion Salad with Rosemary

Having Maine mushrooms available year-round allows you to make this recipe anytime. Oyster Creek Mushrooms, in Damariscotta, Maine, has an assortment of fresh and dried mushrooms. Depending on the season, you might find chanterelles, matsutaki, morelles, or lobster mushrooms overflowing the boxes at their farmer's market display. See page 97 for ordering information.

Serves 6 to 8

7 c mushrooms, reconstituted or fresh (mix and match from the following list for flavor and texture): portobello, matsutake (hen of the woods), cremini, shiitake, maitake (chicken of the woods), morel, lobster

2 T olive oil

1 T unsalted butter

1 red onion, coarsely chopped

2 cloves garlic, crushed (or more, to taste)

3 T fresh rosemary (or 1 T dried)

½ c water

1 T beef or chicken bouillon (I prefer the paste rather than the dried bouillon)

3 T vinegar

1 t salt

1 t white pepper

8 oz feta cheese, crumbled

4 stems of rosemary for garnish

If you are using dried mushrooms, be sure to reconstitute them in plenty of hot water ahead of time. Before you cook, rinse the reconstituted mushrooms and squeeze most of the liquid out of them.

Coarsely chop the mushrooms.

Drizzle the olive oil into a large frying pan or wok. Heat the oil and add the butter. When the butter is melted, add the onion, garlic, and rosemary. Sauté until the onions are lightly golden brown. Add the water, bouillon, and vinegar to the pan and deglaze it. Stir the onions around to dislodge any brown bits from the bottom and sides of the pan. Cook until the water has evaporated and the onions are soft and caramelized.

Add the mushrooms and cook, stirring often, until mushrooms are soft and golden. Add salt, pepper, and feta cheese. Stir and toss to distribute.

This salad is delicious when served warm with grilled steak or chicken, or over baby spinach.

Aroostook County Coleslaw

As a child, I grew up eating the traditional New England Saturday-night supper: baked beans, hot dogs, biscuits with butter and molasses, and fresh coleslaw. It always seemed to fit the bill. Whether it was after a day spent in the snow or at the beach, the flavors always melted in your mouth. This is no ordinary deli coleslaw; the recipe has been evolving for generations. The crisp cabbage, sweet carrots, and a hint of celery are enhanced by my mother's addition of apples. It is often the simplest recipes that taste the best.

Serves 8 to 10

Dressing:
- 1½ c mayonnaise
- 3 T white vinegar
- 3 t celery seed
- 3 T sugar
- 1½ t salt
- ¾ t black pepper
- 2 t Stonewall Kitchen Martini Mustard* or mustard of your choice (optional)

Salad:
- 1 large head green cabbage
- 1 head red cabbage
- 1 lb carrots
- 6 apples (Macintosh, Cortland, and Braeburn are especially nice for this recipe)

Place the mayonnaise in a medium glass or stain-less-steel bowl; add the vinegar, celery seed, sugar, salt and pepper, and mustard (if you desire). Whisk together for one minute. Be sure all of the ingredients are well blended and the sugar is dissolved.

Store in an airtight container in the refrigerator until you are ready to serve.

Wash the vegetables carefully. Cut the core out of the cabbages, separate the leaves, and rinse well. Rinse and peel the carrots. Wash, pare, and core the apples.

Cut apples into ½-inch pieces. Cut all the other vegetables into bite-size pieces, no larger than ¾", to fit easily into your mouth. (Cabbage is notorious for long, stringy pieces that drip dressing on your cheeks, so keep this in mind as you prepare it.) Place the clean, dry vegetables in a beautiful bowl.

Whisk all of the dressing ingredients together well. Pour the dressing onto the vegetables, stirring well to coat evenly.

It is best to make your coleslaw at least an hour or two ahead on the day you plan to serve it. It keeps well only for a day or so.

* See page 97 for ordering information if this product is not available in your local stores.

Pasta Salad with Corn, Black Beans, and Sun-Dried Tomatoes

The flavors of lime and cumin in this refreshing pasta salad give it a Mexican flair. If calories are not an issue, you can serve it with a dollop of sour cream on the side. Spelt is a grain used in place of wheat. You can also use regular semolina pasta in this recipe, if you like. Choose a small pasta shape: bowties, rotini, or penne work well.
Serves 8 to 10

Salad:
 1 lb fresh spelt pasta
 2 T olive oil
 3 ears of fresh sweet corn
 1 yellow bell pepper, chopped
 6 scallions, sliced thin
 16 oz cooked black beans, drained
 8 oz black olives, drained
 10 sun-dried tomato halves packed in oil
 1 jar (8 oz) marinated artichoke hearts
 ½ c Stonewall Kitchen Corn and
   Black Bean Salsa*
 12 sprigs of cilantro
 1 large avocado
 1 T fresh lime juice

Dressing:
 1 bunch fresh cilantro, finely chopped
 ½ c vinegar
 1 c oil

 1 t salt
 1 t pepper
 3 limes, zested and juiced
 3 cloves of garlic, minced
 1 T cumin
 ½ t cayenne

Cook the pasta according to the directions on the package. Drain, and drizzle with 2 T olive oil. Toss to coat, and chill for 30 minutes.

Shuck the corn, and steam or boil until tender (about 6 minutes). Hold the corn vertically on a cutting board and slice off the kernels close to the cob; be careful not to cut into the cob. After the kernels are removed, hold the knife blade perpendicular to the cob and scrape off any little bits of corn left clinging to the cob.

* See page 97 for ordering information if this product is not available in your local stores.

Drain the sun-dried tomatoes and artichoke hearts and slice coarsely. Add all the drained and sliced ingredients to the pasta. Add salsa and toss well. Chill while you prepare dressing and avocado.

In a small bowl, whisk together all the dressing ingredients. Pour over the salad and toss well.

Peel, pit, and slice the avocado. Pour 1 T lime juice over the avocado and toss gently to coat.

Garnish each serving with sprigs of cilantro and a slice or two of avocado.

Tarragon Cucumber Pasta Salad

This cool salad, richly flavored with herbs, is reminiscent of the French countryside. Here in Maine we have so many wonderful herb farms. My favorite is Moose Crossing, located on US Route 1 in Waldoboro. Their greenhouses are overflowing with lush greenery, and their special sections of herbs and edible flowers are tantalizing all summer long. Stop by and visit Ben and his crew. They will surely point you in the right direction.
Serves 6 to 8

Salad:
1 lb pasta (I like to use wheels, rotini, or bowties)
1 T extra virgin olive oil
1 red pepper
5 stalks of celery
2 large tomatoes
1 large cucumber, peeled, seeded, and diced
¼ c fresh parsley, chopped fine
2 T fresh tarragon, chopped fine

Dressing:
½ c garlic or champagne vinegar
1 T fresh squeezed lemon juice
1 t lemon zest
2 T fresh tarragon (or 2 t dried)
1 t fines herbes blend (p. 88)
½ t white pepper
1 t salt
1 T sugar
1 c olive oil

Cook the pasta in salted water until al dente. Drain and toss in a large bowl with 1 T olive oil. Chill while you prepare the vegetables and dressing.

Wash and coarsely chop the pepper, celery, tomatoes, and cucumber. Add the vegetables to the pasta and toss. Add the parsley and tarragon. Toss well. In a small bowl, whisk together the vinegar, lemon juice and zest, more tarragon, fines herbes, salt, pepper, and sugar. Slowly whisk in the olive oil.

Pour the dressing over the salad and toss well. Serve chilled.

APPETIZER AND BRUNCH SALADS

The appetizer sets the tone for your meal. It should be a small serving—just enough to tempt the taste buds, but not so much that your guests are full before they get to the entrée.

Brunch is a delightful way to get your engine geared up for a great day. Make the servings a bit larger than for appetizers, supplement with another tasty item such as rounds of crusty French bread topped with a savory spread, and you have a meal. On pages 41–43 you'll find several excellent recipes for spreads.

The recipes that follow are scintillating. Some are simple, others more complex, but all use fresh ingredients to take advantage of vegetables at the peak of their flavor.

Bacon-Maple Scallops on a Bed of Greens

This dish incorporates several of the delicious tastes of Maine. Searing the scallops ensures that they stay plump and juicy. You may choose to place them on the grill instead of in a pan. Long skewers are great for this.
Serves 6 as an appetizer, 4 for brunch

16 oz (1 lb) large Maine scallops
8 oz thick-cut bacon (or 1 slice per 2 scallops)
½ c Maine maple syrup, divided
1 clove garlic, minced
fresh ground black pepper
sea salt
4 c fresh baby greens, washed and drained

Begin by soaking your bamboo skewers or toothpicks for fifteen minutes in a pie plate filled with room-temperature water. Cut each bacon slice in half so you have two long pieces.

Rinse the scallops, pat them dry, and wrap each with a piece of bacon. Where the two ends of the bacon overlap, push the skewer or toothpick through the overlapped ends of the bacon, then through the entire scallop and out the other side. (If you are using a long skewer, push the skewered scallop down toward one end, leaving the other end free to be used as a long handle.)

Place the wrapped scallops in a clean pie plate and drizzle them with 2 T maple syrup. Sprinkle them with the sea salt and pepper.

Grill or sauté the scallops, ensuring that the bacon is crisp when you're done.

If you are grilling, stay and watch them carefully. Use the top rack, if you can, so the flames will not burn the delicate flesh of the scallops.

If you are sautéing, set the scallops on their sides in the pan. As the bacon cooks, the drippings will begin to coat the scallops. Cook them 3 minutes on each side if they are large—cook only until the scallops are opaque and the bacon is done. Be sure that you give each side, top, and bottom a chance to sear and lightly caramelize. This adds wonderful flavor.

In a small bowl, whisk the remaining maple syrup with the garlic, a sprinkle of sea salt, and a few grinds of black pepper.

Lay out your greens on a platter or on individual plates. Place the scallops on the greens and gently remove the toothpicks. (If you have used skewers, you may leave them in if they are clearly visible.) Drizzle the salad with the maple syrup mixture.

Serve immediately.

Maine Antipasto with Fiddleheads and Smoked Mussels, Salmon, and Trout

This is the epitome of Maine luxury: ocean, woodlands, and farm are combined to mingle smoky, creamy, and pungent flavors.
Serves 6 to 8 as an appetizer, 4 for brunch

1 lb fresh Maine fiddleheads
¼ c balsamic vinegar
½ c olive oil
10 chives, finely chopped
½ t salt
½ t pepper
4 to 6 oz jar of oil packed roasted red peppers
1 lb fresh mozzarella balls packed in oil
4 oz Maine chèvre, flavored or plain
8 oz Maine smoked mussels
8 oz Maine smoked salmon
1 piece (approximately 6 to 8 oz) smoked trout
6 c mesclun greens, washed and drained

Wash and trim the fiddleheads. Steam the fiddleheads in a medium saucepan for three minutes, then rinse immediately with cool water. Place in a resealable plastic bag.

In a small bowl, whisk together vinegar, oil, chives, salt, and pepper. Pour into the bag with the fiddleheads. Set the bag in a bowl and refrigerate for an hour or overnight.

Arrange the greens on a large platter. Mound the marinated fiddleheads in the center. Slice the roasted red peppers into half-inch strips. Drain the mozzarella balls. Break the chèvre and smoked mussels, salmon, and trout into large chunks. Lay the roasted red pepper strips around the fiddleheads and arrange the other items around the edges.

Serve immediately with bread rounds or crackers if you like. Set out a dish of your favorite dressing on the side.

Spicy Tuna Wrappers on Romaine Lettuce

Here is an interesting alternative to traditional sushi. Whenever you purchase fish for a sushi dish, be *sure* it is fresh. Simpson's Seafood on US Route 1 in Wiscasset, Maine, is one of those places where you can always find the freshest, most delicious fish. The rice wrappers (sometimes labeled "spring roll skins") can be found in larger grocery stores and Asian markets. When soaked they quickly become pliable and ready to use. *Serves 10 as a light appetizer or 2 for brunch*

½ c mayonnaise
¼ c chili paste (sambal oelek)
1 lb *fresh* sushi-grade tuna
15 romaine lettuce leaves
¼ of a 10.5 oz package bean thread noodles, approximately
10 rice paper wrappers, 8¾" in diameter
1 T wasabi
¼ c pickled ginger
20 fresh basil leaves

In a small bowl, mix the mayonnaise and the chili paste. Set aside.

Slice the tuna very thin across the grain. Arrange on a plate, cover, and chill.

Separate the leafy parts of the romaine from the thick center rib on five of the leaves. Tear the leafy parts into large 1-inch strips but leave the ribs whole. Save the remaining whole leaves for your platter.

Soak the bean thread noodles in warm water

until reconstituted. Drain.

Have yourself ready to roll, with your ingredients set out within easy reach around your work surface. Arrange in order: dry rice wrappers, a pie plate half full of warm water, wasabi, mayonnaise/chili paste mixture, pickled ginger, prepared romaine ribs and leaves, sliced tuna, basil, and bean thread noodles.

Slide a rice wrapper into the warm water and let it sit for 20 seconds or until soft. Let it drip dry and lay it on your work surface. Blot with a paper towel to remove excess moisture.

Spread a scant ¼ t (or more, if you like your wrappers spicy) of wasabi down the center of the wrapper. Spread a teaspoon of the mayonnaise mixture over that. Lay a few pieces of ginger on the mayonnaise. Place a romaine rib and a couple of leaf pieces on next. Top the lettuce with a few slices of tuna.

Pinch a small bunch of noodles in your fingers and lay them on the tuna. Put two basil leaves on top.

Roll up the wrap: Start at one side and fold it over the fillings. Fold each end toward the center, then roll it up the rest of the way. Make sure all of the fillings are enclosed in the wrapper. It works well to roll them tightly, but not so tight that they rip.

To serve, cut each roll in half on a diagonal and arrange them on top of the large leaves of romaine lettuce. You can set out dishes with a dollop of the mayonnaise/chili mixture, or soy sauce and wasabi for dunking the rolls as you nibble.

Shrimp Salad with Chili-Lime Dressing

Here is a delicious combination of shrimp cocktail and green salad. Take the spice to your limit!
Serves 8 as an appetizer, 4 for brunch

Dressing:
2 t Tabasco sauce or Asian chili paste
½ c ketchup
1 lime, zested and juiced
2 ribs celery, from the heart, finely chopped
1 yellow or orange bell pepper,
   seeded and finely chopped
2 to 3 T parsley leaves, chopped fine
fresh ground black pepper to taste

Salad:
2 lbs cooked Maine shrimp
8 large lettuce leaves

Devein the shrimp, if necessary.

Combine hot pepper sauce, ketchup, lime zest and juice, celery, bell pepper, and parsley in a small bowl. Stir. Add fresh ground black pepper to taste. Add shrimp and coat evenly.

Chill at least 20 minutes, then line 4 cocktail glasses or small dishes with lettuce leaves, and top each with chilled shrimp.

Baby Spinach with Bacon, Cheddar, and Midcoast Mediterranean Dressing

Here is a combination of flavors that mingle with bacon and cheese to create a delicious spinach salad.
Serves 4 to 6

Salad:
- 6 c baby spinach
- 4 hard-boiled eggs
- 8 oz Maine cheddar cheese
- 8 strips bacon

Dressing:
- 2 T white vinegar
- 4 T bacon fat
- 1 T fresh oregano, chopped
- 1 clove garlic, minced
- 1 t pure Maine maple syrup
- ¼ t salt
- ½ t white pepper
- 2 T fresh parsley, chopped

½ c fresh Maine apples, cored and chopped

Wash the spinach. Fry the bacon until crisp. Remove from pan and drain on paper towels. Reserve 4 T of the bacon fat.

Peel and rinse the hard-boiled eggs and cut them into quarters. Slice the cheese into bite-size chunks.

To serve the salads, evenly distribute the spinach on four individual chilled glass plates. Crumble two pieces of bacon on top of each. Add four quarters of egg. Sprinkle cheese on top.

In a small bowl, whisk together the dressing ingredients until well blended. Drizzle the dressing over each salad to your taste.

Sprinkle with apples and enjoy.

Baby Spinach with Rosemary Chèvre and Blueberry Vinaigrette

The delicate leaves of baby spinach meet the sweetness of Maine blueberries. This is the perfect post–farmer's market lunch. It's quick, easy, and delicious.
Serves 4 to 6

Salad:

6 c baby spinach
2 c shredded carrots
4 oz rosemary chèvre
1 pint wild Maine blueberries
¼ c dried blueberries
½ c dried cherries

Dressing:

½ c blueberry vinegar (p. 85)
2 T fresh rosemary, chopped
1 t sugar or Splenda sweetener
½ t salt
½ t fresh ground pepper
1 clove garlic, minced
1 T Raye's Fall Harvest Mustard* (whole-seed mustard blended with cranberries)
½ c olive oil

Wash the fruit and vegetables. Place the spinach, carrots, blueberries (both fresh and dried), and dried cherries in a large bowl.

In a medium bowl, whisk together vinegar, rosemary, sugar, salt, pepper, garlic, and mustard. Slowly whisk in the oil.

Gently toss the salad ingredients together. Crumble the chèvre and add to the greens.

Dress the salad to your taste and serve immediately. This is very nice with a piece of rosemary foccacia (p. 92).

* See page 97 for ordering information if this product is not available in your local stores.

Marinated Shrimp Salad with Lime and Radicchio

This light and zesty shrimp dish is wonderful for a sophisticated dinner party or a summer barbecue. The seafood is marinated in a lime dressing to enhance its fresh taste. Served on a bed of greens, it is a perfect blend of flavor and texture.
Serves 6 as an appetizer or 4 for brunch

Dressing / Marinade:
  2 T fresh lime juice
  2 T white vinegar
  2 T tequila
  2 T red onion, minced
  3 T fresh cilantro, minced
  2 T each red, orange, and yellow
    peppers, minced
  ¼ c Roma tomatoes, minced
  4 dashes of Tabasco
  ½ t salt
  ¾ t black pepper (or a pinch of crushed
    red pepper flakes, if you prefer)

6 c blanched Maine shrimp (just barely
  cooked and tender)

Salad:
  3 heads radicchio
  1 head endive
  ¼ c fresh grated Asiago cheese
  2 heads Bibb or Boston lettuce
  whole pieces of chive or cilantro for garnish

Place the lime juice in a medium glass or stainless-steel bowl. Add the vinegar, tequila, onion, cilantro, peppers, tomatoes, Tabasco, salt, and pepper. Whisk together for one minute, ensuring that all of the ingredients are well blended.

Add shrimp and toss lightly. Store in an airtight container in the refrigerator until you are ready to serve.

Wash the vegetables carefully. Cut the core out

of the radicchio, separate the leaves, and rinse well. While you may keep the smaller leaves of lettuce and endive whole, tear the bigger leaves into small strips (remembering that all pieces should fit easily into your mouth). Place the clean, dry vegetables in a large bowl and toss well.

When you are ready to serve, lay your greens out on a beautiful platter (or individual dishes, if you like). Carefully spoon shrimp out onto the vegetables in an even layer, mounding them slightly in the center. Stir the remaining dressing left in the container, and drizzle it over the shrimp and vegetables.

Sprinkle the Asiago cheese over the shrimp. Garnish with the whole chives or cilantro.

Wait to assemble the salad until the last minute, as it looks best when presented immediately after you plate it.

Warm Greens with Pears, Pecans, and Goat Cheese

Many fancy restaurants have their own versions of this simple and delicious recipe. Add vegetables (grape tomatoes, celery, endive, or artichoke hearts, to name a few) as you like to give it your own special flair.
Serves 6 as an appetizer, 4 for brunch

Salad:
6 c baby mesclun greens
3 baby Vidalia onions
1 c pecans
2 ripe Anjou pears
1 T lemon juice
6 to 8 oz chèvre

Dressing:
2 T fresh lemon juice
2 T balsamic vinaigrette
4 T olive oil
½ t salt
½ t fresh ground pepper
1 t sugar or Splenda sweetener

Wash and dry the greens, and place them in a large bowl. Wash, trim, and slice the baby Vidalia onions and add to the greens. Add pecans to the mixture.

Rinse, core, and coarsely chop the pears. Toss with 1 T lemon juice. Add pears to the greens.

Crumble the chèvre into ½-inch chunks, and toss with the mixture.

In a small saucepan, heat the dressing ingredients. When warm, pour over the salad and toss. The greens will wilt and the chèvre will begin to soften.

Serve immediately.

Gazpacho Garden Salad

Children love to create this pretty layered salad. They enjoy making patterns with the different colors. When you serve, make sure each person gets a little of every color.
Serves 6 to 8

Dressing:

½ c extra virgin olive oil

⅓ c lemon juice

2 cloves garlic, minced

2 T tomato paste

1½ t salt

¼ t fresh ground pepper

1 shallot, peeled and minced

Salad:

1 medium green bell pepper, seeded and diced small

1 medium red bell pepper, seeded and diced small

1 medium orange bell pepper, seeded and diced small

1 medium yellow bell pepper, seeded and diced small

3 large, firm tomatoes, diced small

1 large cucumber, peeled, seeded, and diced small

½ c thinly sliced scallions

1 bunch parsley, chopped fine

1 Vidalia onion, chopped (about 1 c)

In a 1-pint jar with a tight-fitting lid, combine oil, lemon juice, garlic, tomato paste, salt, pepper, and shallot; shake well.

Wash and chop the vegetables, keeping each type separate.

In a straight-sided glass container, layer half of the chopped peppers, tomato, and cucumber, arranging the layers to show off the contrasting colors. Repeat layers using the remaining peppers, tomato, and cucumber.

Top with the scallions and parsley. Pour dressing over salad. Chill for 4 hours to blend flavors.

Bar Harbor Salad with Blueberry-Maple Dressing

Two special northern New England delights marry to create this delicate dish. A touch of maple syrup with the sweet/tang of fresh Maine blueberries make this salad perfect for young and old palates alike.
Serves 4

Dressing:
½ c blueberry vinegar (p. 85, or see below)
½ c olive oil
½ c vegetable oil
½ c pure Maine maple syrup
2 T Stonewall Kitchen Cranberry Mustard*
salt to taste
2 T chopped chives
fresh ground black pepper

Salad:
3 c Boston lettuce, washed and dried
3 c red lettuce, washed and dried
4 T blue cheese or Roquefort
6 red onions, sliced into ¼-inch rings
4 T toasted macadamia nuts or walnuts
½ c fresh Maine blueberries

In a medium bowl, whisk all dressing ingredients together to blend. Chill while you are preparing the salad.

Put lettuces in a nonreactive bowl and drizzle with dressing until lettuce is thinly coated. Divide lettuce evenly among 4 individual salad plates. Top each salad with an even distribution of onion rings, blue cheese, walnuts, and blueberries.

To toast the nuts, break them up into coarse chunks and place in a single layer on a cookie sheet. Heat in preheated 350°F oven for about 5 minutes.

Quick Blueberry Vinegar
Here's a fast and easy shortcut for making blueberry vinegar. Mix equal proportions of Wyman's blueberry juice* with white vinegar and let the mixture sit in the refrigerator overnight. Use it just like regular vinegar in recipes of your choice.

See page 97 for ordering information if this product is not available in your local stores.

Irresistible Caesar Salad

F ast, fresh, and fantastic. Please your family and your friends with this simple yet dazzling recipe, which even my children love! When I first made this salad for friends, they came back with their bread to scoop out any leftover dribbles of dressing from the empty bowl. The dressing and croutons can both be prepared ahead of time.
Serves 8 to 10

Dressing:
2 lemons
1 anchovy, or ¼ to ½ t anchovy paste
2 T minced garlic
1 T Raye's Sweet and Spicy Mustard*
1 T cider vinegar
3 dashes Tabasco
3 dashes Worcestershire sauce
1 t Maine maple syrup
6 to 8 oz extra virgin olive oil
½ c freshly grated Parmesan cheese
¼ t salt
½ t fresh cracked black pepper

In a medium glass or stainless-steel bowl, juice the lemons. Add the anchovy, garlic, mustard, vinegar, Tabasco, Worcestershire sauce, and maple syrup. Whisk together for one minute. Be sure all of the ingredients are well blended.

Slowly drizzle the oil into the bowl as you whisk. Continue whisking until all of the oil is incorporated.

Whisk in the Parmesan cheese, salt, and pepper. Store in an airtight container in the refrigerator until you are ready to serve.

Croutons:
1 loaf of bread (pumpernickel, crusty baguette, or whatever you have on hand)
⅓ c butter
1 t garlic powder
¼ t fresh cracked black pepper
dash salt

Preheat the oven to 350°F. Cut the loaf of bread into ¾-inch cubes and place in a large bowl. Melt the butter and stir in the garlic, pepper, and salt. Pour the butter mixture over the bread cubes and toss to coat all pieces evenly.

Arrange a cooling rack on top of a cookie sheet and place the bread cubes on the rack. Toast in a preheated oven for 6 to 9 minutes.

Remove from oven and cool. Croutons can be stored in a plastic bag or airtight container in the freezer for several months.

See page 97 for ordering information if this product is not available in your local stores.

Salad:
   3 heads of romaine lettuce
   ⅓ c freshly grated Parmesan cheese
   3 hard-boiled eggs, peeled and chopped
      (or use three raw egg yolks, if you prefer)

Wash the lettuce and tear into bite-size pieces (re-member—not pieces that you have to fold twice before they will fit into your mouth). Place the clean, dry lettuce in a beautiful bowl.

Just before you serve, whisk or shake the dressing well. Drizzle the dressing onto the greens. Add the Parmesan cheese, chopped (or raw) eggs, and croutons. Toss well to coat all of the lettuce evenly with the dressing.

This salad looks beautiful with the addition of a head of chopped radicchio tossed in with the final ingredients. For a heartier meal, add grilled mari-nated chicken, shrimp, or steak.

Tomato and Mozzarella Salad

Wonderfully colorful, this salad is great for entertaining because it is assembled several hours or a day in advance.
Serves 8

Dressing:
   ½ c olive oil
   ¼ c balsamic vinegar
   2 T herb mixture, or basil, chopped fine
   1 handful fresh parsley, coarsely chopped

Salad:
   2 c Roma tomatoes, chopped coarse
   1 c green or yellow bell pepper,
      chopped coarse
   1 c seeded cucumber, chopped coarse
   1 c broccoli florets
   1 c cauliflower florets
   1 c sweet red or Vidalia onion, thinly sliced
   1 c celery, chopped fine
   1 cup carrots, thinly sliced

   10 fresh large basil leaves
   1 lb marinated small mozzarella balls,
      or mozzarella cheese

Place the dressing ingredients in a large bowl. Whisk together until completely mixed.

Wash and chop the vegetables. Add all of the vegetables and cheese to the bowl. Toss with the dressing and let marinate in the fridge overnight.

Serve with fresh crusty bread dipped in a drizzle of garlic oil.

Clockwise from three o'clock: Easy Olive Tapenade; Crabmeat and Artichoke Spread with Sun-Dried Tomatoes; Kitchen Garden Herbed Cheese Spread; Roasted Garlic Blue Cheese Spread, Smoked Salmon Pâté; Garden Cheddar Spread.

SPREADS TO COMPLEMENT YOUR SALADS

For an easy light brunch, accompany your featured salad with one or more of these tasty spreads served atop fresh-baked bread, toasted French bread rounds, bagels, panini, crackers, or melba toast.

Kitchen Garden Herbed Cheese Spread

Best made a day ahead so the flavors can dance around a bit.
Serves 4 to 6

8 oz Neufchatel or regular cream cheese
8 oz plain chèvre
1 T fresh rosemary, chopped
¼ c fresh parsley, minced
¼ c fresh chives, minced

optional: minced fresh oregano, thyme, marjoram, or sage to taste
½ t garlic powder or 1 clove fresh garlic, minced
½ t white pepper
½ t salt

Blend all together until smooth. Chill for 30 minutes or overnight.

Easy Olive Tapenade

Serves 4 to 6

12 to 16 oz black or green pitted olives

In a food processor, pulse the olives until they are finely ground and pieces are uniform in size, like coarse sand. Keep in a covered container in your refrigerator. Flavor is best if used within two weeks.

Smoked Salmon Pâté

Serves 6 to 8

8 oz smoked salmon
8 oz Neufchatel or cream cheese
2 T fresh dill, minced
juice of ½ lemon
dash of white pepper
1 T capers, for garnish

In the bowl of a food processor place the salmon, cream cheese, dill, lemon juice, and pepper. Pulse until the mixture is well blended.

Scoop into a decorative bowl and cover with plastic wrap. Chill for 30 minutes. Garnish with capers before serving.

Can also be served warm: Spread on thick slices of bread and broil for two minutes, or until bubbly.

Crabmeat and Artichoke Spread with Sun-Dried Tomatoes

This simple recipe is often served as a dip. For a crunchy variation, add a small can of chopped water chestnuts (drained).
Serves 6 to 8

1 lb fresh Maine lump crabmeat
8 oz marinated artichoke hearts, chopped
   fine
1 c mayonnaise
1 c sour cream
1 c freshly grated Parmesan cheese
6 sun-dried tomato halves packed in oil,
   chopped fine
6 scallions, minced

½ t white pepper
dash Tabasco sauce
1 T butter or olive oil spray
   (to grease baking dish)

In a non-reactive bowl, place the mayonnaise, sour cream, Parmesan cheese, sun dried tomatoes, scallions, pepper, and Tabasco. Mix well. Fold in the artichoke hearts. Gently fold in the crabmeat.

Place into a greased 2-qt baking dish. Cover and bake 25 minutes in a 325°F oven. Spread on bread rounds or crackers.

The mixture also can be made a day ahead and kept in the refrigerator until you are ready to bake it.

Garden Cheddar Spread

Delicious on whole-grain bread, this mixture can also be used as a dip for raw veggies or crackers.
Serves 4 to 6

8 oz cream cheese
¼ c soft butter
3 T milk
1 T Raye's Sweet & Spicy Mustard*
1 c Maine cheddar cheese, finely shredded
3 scallions, washed, trimmed,
   and thinly sliced
¼ c carrots, finely shredded
1 t Tabasco sauce

Blend together cream cheese and butter. Add milk and mustard. Stir in cheddar cheese and half of the scallions. Mix in carrots and Tabasco. Blend well, making sure there are no lumps. Garnish with the remaining scallions when serving.

* *See page 97 for ordering information if not available in your local stores.*

Roasted Garlic Blue Cheese Spread

Also delicious melted atop grilled steak or fish.
Serves 4 to 6

5 slices bacon
16 oz Neufchatel cheese
1 stick butter, softened
1 t salt
1 t pepper
3 T roasted garlic purée
12 oz blue cheese, crumbled

Cook bacon until light brown and crispy. Drain on a plate lined with paper towels.
  Blend together the Neufchatel cheese and butter. Add the salt, pepper, and roasted garlic.

Blend again until smooth. Add the blue cheese, mixing until well incorporated.
  This spread will keep in the refrigerator for 2 to 3 days, or can be frozen.

To roast garlic: Cut the top quarter off of a head of garlic to expose the tops of the cloves. Place in a foil-lined baking dish and drizzle heavily with olive oil. Bake for 50 minutes at 300°F. Remove from oven and let sit until cool enough to handle. Squeeze the now very soft cloves out of the garlic skins into a dish. (Save the skins for making soup stock and the garlic-flavored oil from the bottom of the dish to use in other recipes.)

DINNER SALADS

When we sit down to eat a healthy meal full of flavors both bold and delicate, we not only satisfy the growling in our stomachs, but also add to the contentment and peacefulness we feel. Mealtime gives us a moment to contemplate the many rich experiences we enjoy every day, allowing us to move forward with a smile.

Marinated Steak Salad with Oranges and Capers

Flank steak is a tender cut of beef that is sliced on the diagonal across the grain. When it is marinated and grilled to medium rare, it melts in your mouth. Wolfe's Neck Farm, located in Freeport, Maine, is one of the premier purveyors of beef in its healthiest state. If you cannot find their flank steak, use the best you can find from your local butcher. Be sure it is fresh and as organic as possible. You will be surprised at the difference in taste. It's worth the effort.
Serves 4 to 6

2 lbs Wolfe's Neck Farm sirloin or flank steak*
1 T fresh ground peppercorns
2 cloves garlic, minced
2 T Raye's Bar Harbor Real Ale Mustard*
2 T olive oil

Salad:
　1 large ripe red or orange bell pepper, chopped into ¾-inch chunks
　1 c grape tomatoes
　¼ c drained small capers
　1 small red onion, chopped coarse
　2 large navel oranges, segmented

Dressing:
　¼ c red wine vinegar
　¾ c olive oil
　2 T frozen orange juice concentrate
　¼ t Tabasco sauce or chili paste
　1 clove garlic, minced
　½ t salt
　½ t white pepper

1 large head red leaf lettuce, washed and torn in to bite-size pieces

　See page 97 for ordering information.

Mix together the pepper, garlic, mustard, and olive oil. Rub steak all over with this mixture; cover, and let the meat sit at room temperature for an hour.

Grill the steak to your liking just before you serve the salad. Slice the steak on an angle into thin strips, and cover with foil until you are ready to serve.

To segment the oranges: Cut a slice off of the top and bottom of the fruit. Remove the peel by slicing down the sides of the orange, turning it each time you cut. Slice through the peel and white pith, leaving the segments visible. Insert your knife along either side of each membrane. The segments will slide out as they are trimmed. Be sure there is no white pith or membrane remaining on the segments. Once all of the segments have been removed, squeeze the remaining center portion of the orange over the vegetables to release any juice.

Gently toss the peppers, tomatoes, capers, onion, and orange segments together.

Whisk the vinegar, oil, orange juice concentrate, Tabasco, and garlic together. Add salt and pepper. Drizzle the dressing over the vegetable mixture and toss again.

Place the torn lettuce on a large platter. Gently mound the salad on top of the lettuce. Lay the steak strips over the top. Lightly drizzle all with dressing and serve the remaining dressing on the side.

Traditional Maine Lobster Salad

There is no place in the world better than Maine to enjoy the flavors of traditional lobster salad. While there are many variations, it's hard to beat the tried-and-true simplicity of this recipe.
Serves 2 to 4

1 lb fresh cooked Maine lobster meat
½ c mayonnaise
¼ t salt
½ t fresh ground pepper
½ c celery, finely chopped

Coarsely chop the lobster, being sure to check for shells and cartilage. In a medium bowl, place the remaining ingredients. Stir well.

Add the lobster, stirring gently to coat the meat.

Serve on a bed of greens with a slice of lemon, or on a fresh baked roll to eat as a sandwich.

Country Ham Salad Served with Corn Fritters

Whenever we have a big ham dinner, I trim the tender bits off of the bone to make this salad. It is delicious on a bed of greens, accompanied by fresh corn fritters. (When fresh corn is not available, try serving this salad in a pita pocket or mounded on a slice of homemade anadama bread.)
Serves 6

Dressing:
   3 T Raye's Aroostook Gold Mustard*
   2 T heavy cream
   2 t fresh tarragon, minced
   2 T fresh parsley, minced
   2 T cider vinegar (or pickle juice)
   ½ c olive oil

Salad:
   1 lb of ham, chunked into small pieces
   8 oz. Maine cheddar cheese (or fresh
      mozzarella), chunked into small pieces
   2 large stalks of celery, chopped fine
   1 scallion, sliced thin
   4 c of your choice of greens: spring mix,
      mesclun, or leaf lettuce
   1 extra scallion, sliced thin, for garnish

In a medium mixing bowl, place the mustard, heavy cream, tarragon, and parsley, mixing well.

Whisk in the cider vinegar until well blended. Slowly whisk in the oil until the dressing is thickened.

Add the ham, cheese, celery, and scallion. Toss with the dressing until all are well coated.

Serve over a bed of greens of your choice, garnished with scallion. For a heartier meal, add corn fritters on the side. (Recipe on next page.)

 * *See page 97 for ordering information if this product is not available in your local stores.*

Corn Fritters:
vegetable oil, for frying
¾ c King Arthur all-purpose flour
½ t Bakewell Cream (or cream of tartar)
½ t baking soda
½ t salt
⅛ t nutmeg
2 t sugar or Splenda sweetener
2 T water
2 c fresh corn kernels
2 eggs
sea salt, to taste
fresh ground black pepper to taste
cayenne pepper (optional) to taste

Fill a large, heavy-bottomed saucepan with 3 inches of vegetable oil and heat to medium-high heat. Nearby, place a plate lined with paper towels where you will drain the fritters when they come out of the hot oil.

Combine the flour, Bakewell Cream, baking soda, salt, nutmeg, and sugar in one bowl. In a separate bowl, whisk the eggs and water together. Mix wet ingredients into dry, stirring until just mixed, but not lumpy. The batter will be thick. Add the corn and stir gently until well combined.

When the oil is ready for frying, drop in spoonfuls of the batter and fry on all sides until golden brown and puffy. This should take no more than 3 to 4 minutes. Remove fritters with a slotted spoon or tongs and drain on the paper towel–lined plate.

Serve the fritters while they are still hot and crispy, sprinkling with sea salt, pepper, and cayenne to suit individual tastes.

These little fritters are best when they are first made, but you can store leftovers in the refrigerator and reheat in a 350°F oven for 20 minutes.

Maine-Style Chef's Salad

Traditional chef's salads are made with cold cuts and thinly sliced cheeses. Here we have a delightful twist on that old favorite: the luscious tastes of the Maine coast—shrimp, smoked salmon, and lobster—combined with fresh peapods, beets, carrots, and local cheeses. Remember to snitch a bite or two for yourself as you create this masterpiece of delicacies.
Serves 6 to 8

Salad Vegetables:
  6 c mesclun greens
  2 c baby spinach
  1 c baby carrots
  2 c fresh snow peas
  1 lb fresh asparagus
  3 large portobello mushroom caps
  1 c sliced cooked beets (optional)

Dressing:
  4 T balsamic vinegar
  4 T olive oil
  ¼ c chives, chopped
  1 clove garlic, minced
  ½ t salt
  ½ t pepper

Seafoods and Cheeses:
  1 lb clean fresh cooked Maine lobster meat
  1 lb fresh cooked Maine shrimp
  8 oz smoked salmon
  4 oz Mystique Cheese Rosemary Chèvre*
  4 oz Mystique Cheese Herb Chèvre*

Wash the mesclun greens and baby spinach and place them on a large platter (or on individual salad plates, if you prefer).

Quarter the baby carrots lengthwise to create long, thick matchsticks. Trim the ends off the snow peas.

* See page 96 for ordering information if this product is not available in your local stores.

Trim the bottom ends off of the asparagus. Blanch the asparagus in boiling salted water for 3 minutes. Remove and rinse with cold water. Set aside.

Lightly wash the portobello mushroom caps and slice into ½-inch strips.

In a small bowl, whisk together vinegar, olive oil, chives, garlic, salt, and pepper. Place the mushroom slices in a large resealable plastic bag and pour the dressing over the mushrooms. Set the bag in a bowl and chill while you assemble the salad.

Arrange the lobster, shrimp, smoked salmon, chèvre, carrots, snow peas, asparagus, and beets (if desired) on top of the greens. You can be creative here, arranging the ingredients decoratively (for example, like the spokes of a wheel).

Drain the mushrooms carefully into a bowl, reserving the dressing. Place the mushrooms on the greens.

Drizzle the dressing over all of the ingredients. There should be just a touch on the seafood and vegetables, allowing the flavor of each element to come through.

Serve chilled with breadsticks or rosemary foccacia (see p. 92).

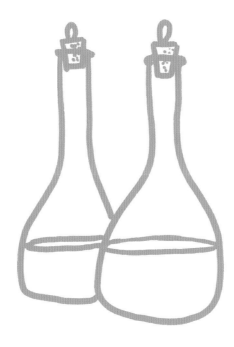

Duck Salad with Blueberries and Walnut Vinaigrette

The moist, dark duck breast is complemented by the fruit and nuts in this recipe. The walnut vinaigrette has many layers of flavor, and by dressing the salad lightly you will create a dish that's both healthful and tasty.
Serves 4 to 6

Salad:

3 whole duck breasts
¼ c Wyman's Maine blueberry juice*
1 T lemon juice
2 fresh ripe peaches
2 fresh ripe Anjou pears
1 yellow bell pepper
1 red bell pepper
3 stalks of celery
½ c chopped walnuts
⅛ c slivered almonds
1 pint fresh Maine blueberries
½ c Maine Munchies dried Maine blueberries*

Dressing:

½ c raspberry vinegar
½ c walnut oil
½ c olive oil
1 T sugar or Splenda sweetener
1 t salt
1 t fresh ground pepper

4 to 6 c fresh greens of your choice

Poach or grill the duck breasts until they are cooked through. Remove the skin and coarsely chop the meat. Place the cooked duck in a resealable plastic bag and pour the blueberry juice over the top. Chill while you prepare the salad.

Wash the fruit and vegetables. Peel, core, seed, and coarsely chop the peaches, pears, peppers, and celery. Place them in a large bowl. Sprinkle with the lemon juice and toss.

Add the walnuts, almonds, both fresh and dried blueberries, and duck. Toss to mix.

In a small bowl, whisk together the dressing ingredients. Pour over the salad and toss.

Serve on a bed of greens.

* See pages 96 and 97 for ordering information if this product is not available in your local stores.

Asparagus, Chicken, and Pasta Salad with Hazelnuts

L ook for the asparagus, eggs, chicken, and
parsley at a farmers' market near you.
Serves 4

1 quart chicken broth
2 c chunked chicken
3 T fresh lemon juice
salt and fresh ground pepper to taste
3 T vegetable oil
3 T hazelnut oil
8 oz penne pasta
1¼ lb asparagus, peeled and trimmed
½ c roasted red peppers
2 hard-boiled eggs, peeled and chopped
4 T fresh parsley, chopped
⅓ c toasted hazelnuts

Bring chicken broth to a boil in a medium pot. Add chicken and poach until cooked through, approximately 15 minutes. Remove chicken; cool until it is easy to handle.

In a large bowl, whisk lemon, salt, pepper, and oils. Add chicken.

Bring a large pot of salted water to a boil. Cook penne uncovered approximately 9 minutes, or until al dente. Drain. Rinse briefly with cold water to stop the cooking process.

Cut the asparagus into 1½-inch lengths. Add to the chicken stock. Cook over high heat for 2 minutes, or until crisp-tender. Rinse with cold water. Reserve 12 tips for garnish.

Slice roasted red peppers into thin strips.

Add pasta, asparagus, and roasted red peppers to chicken mixture. Toss well. Taste and adjust seasonings to your liking. Add hard-boiled eggs and toss lightly.

You can keep this in the refrigerator for a day, but bring it to room temperature before you serve it. Spoon salad onto plates and garnish with asparagus tips, parsley, and toasted hazelnuts.

Grilled Chicken over Down East Asian Salad Served with Scallion Beignets

*T*his recipe can be made using steak instead of chicken. It is also wonderful with fresh seafood tossed in. The dressing can be mild or spicy, as you like, to enhance the delicious Asian flavors that mingle in this dish. Scallion Beignets, savory little fritters, are a perfect complement.
Serves 6

Chicken:
- 1½ lb boneless chicken breast or thighs
- 1 T grated fresh ginger
- 1 T garlic, minced
- 1 T soy sauce
- 1 T sesame oil
- 1 T fresh lemon juice
- 1 t to 1 T chili paste

Dressing:
- 2 T garlic, minced
- 2 T grated fresh ginger root
- ½ c ginger or white vinegar
- 1 T sugar, honey, or Splenda sweetener
- ¼ c soy sauce
- 1 T molasses
- 2 T sesame oil
- 6 oz extra virgin olive oil
- ½ t salt
- ½ t fresh cracked black pepper
- 1 t (or 1 T) chili paste to taste

Salad:
- 1 napa or Chinese cabbage
- 1 bok choy cabbage
- 1 head radicchio
- 1 large daikon radish
- 3 medium carrots
- 1 bunch of scallions
- 1 10-oz package Chinese crunchy noodles

Cut the chicken into chunks and place in a resealable plastic bag. Add the fresh ginger, garlic, soy sauce, sesame oil, lemon, and chili paste. Seal the bag and rub the marinade into the chicken. Let sit in the refrigerator for 30 minutes, or as long as overnight.

Grill or stir-fry the chicken until completely cooked. Chill while you are assembling the salad.

In a medium glass or stainless-steel bowl, place the garlic, ginger, vinegar, sugar, soy sauce, molasses, chili paste, salt, and pepper. Whisk together for one minute. Be sure all of the ingredients are well blended and the sugar is dissolved.

Slowly drizzle the sesame oil and the olive oil into the bowl as you whisk. Continue whisking until all of the oil is incorporated. Store in an airtight container in the refrigerator until you are ready to serve.

Be sure to use a completely clean cutting board when you start this phase. Wash the vegetables carefully. Cut the core out of the cabbages, separate the leaves, and rinse well. Peel and julienne the daikon radish and carrots, making pieces the size of matchsticks.

Cut the root end off of each scallion, discarding any discolored layers. Slice the scallions into ¼-inch pieces.

Cut all of the other vegetables into bite-size pieces, no larger than 1 inch. Place the clean, dry vegetables in a beautiful bowl. (If necessary, they can be stored in the refrigerator in an airtight container or resealable plastic bags overnight.)

Just before you serve, whisk or shake the dressing well. Drizzle the dressing onto the veggies, tossing well to coat all pieces evenly. Add the chicken pieces and toss again.

At the very last minute, add the crunchy noodles. Toss and serve as soon as possible, as this salad will begin to wilt if it sits too long.

Scallion Beignets:

6 c vegetable oil or Crisco, for frying
1 c King Arthur all-purpose flour
½ t Bakewell Cream or cream of tartar
½ t baking soda
½ t salt
½ cup water
8 to 10 scallions, cleaned, dried, trimmed, and chopped
¼ t cayenne pepper
½ t salt
fresh ground black pepper

Fill a large heavy-bottomed saucepan with 3 inches of vegetable oil and heat to medium-high heat. Arrange a plate lined with paper towels on the counter where you will drain the beignets when they come out of the hot oil.

Combine the dry ingredients in a bowl. Add the water. The batter will be thick. Add the chopped scallions and season with the cayenne, salt, and black pepper. When the oil is ready for frying, drop spoonfuls of the batter into the oil and fry on all sides until golden brown and puffy. This should take no more than 3 to 4 minutes.

Remove the browned fritters and drain them on the paper towel–lined plate. Season with salt, and serve immediately while they are still hot and crispy.

These little treats are best when they are first made. Store leftovers in the refrigerator. Reheat them in a 350°F oven for 20 minutes before serving.

Greens with Herbed Chicken and Asiago

Fresh herbs are available all summer long. Find your favorite organic garden center and purchase herbs in pots to plant at home. There is nothing like going out to your own kitchen garden to snip greens for your dinner. Start this recipe several hours or a day before you plan to serve it, as the chicken strips need to be marinated.
Serves 4

Herb Oil Marinade:
1 t fresh summer savory, minced (or 1/2 t dried)
1 T fresh thyme, minced (or 1 t dried)
1½ T fresh sage, minced (or 1 t dried)
1½ T fresh rosemary, minced (or 1 t dried)
1 t fresh marjoram, minced (or 1/4 t dried)
6 T fresh parsley, minced (or 2 T dried)
2 cloves garlic, minced
1 T fresh lemon zest, minced
pinch of ground allspice

½ t cayenne pepper
1 t salt
½ t pepper
¾ c olive oil

4 boneless chicken breast halves

* See page 97 for ordering information if this product is not available in your local stores.

Dressing:
½ of herb oil marinade mixture
juice of 2 lemons
¼ c fresh grated Asiago cheese
2 T Raye's Lemon Pepper Mustard*
1 shallot, minced
1 T sugar or Splenda sweetener

Salad:
10 fresh basil leaves, chopped fine
1 orange or yellow bell pepper, seeded and
   sliced (or coarsely chopped)
Two large handfuls frisée lettuce or baby
   mesclun greens
1 head of Boston lettuce, washed and torn into
   bite-size pieces
¼ c fresh grated Asiago cheese for garnish

In a bowl, combine all herb oil marinade ingredients and mix well. Divide into two parts. Save one half of the herb oil in a glass jar or bottle and keep refrigerated until ready to use in the salad dressing. Use the other half to marinate the chicken.

Slice the chicken breasts into large strips. Toss pieces in the herb oil marinade. Cover the chicken and chill for several hours or overnight to marinate.

When you are ready to cook the meat, discard the marinade and grill or sauté the strips of chicken until they are cooked through.

Make dressing for salad: To the reserved half of the herb oil mixture add the lemon juice, Asiago cheese, mustard, shallot, and sugar. Cover and shake to emulsify.

Toss the greens and peppers together with this dressing and place on serving dish(es). Arrange chicken pieces on top, drizzle with more of the dressing, sprinkle with 1/4 cup of Asiago cheese, and serve.

Pasta Salad with Champagne Dill Mustard Dressing Served with Olive-Cheese Nuggets

This pasta salad can be made with wheat, spelt, jerusalem artichoke-, or spinach-based noodles. I like to use small shapes so they catch the dressing and are easy to chew. Rotini, penne, small shells, and wagon wheels are fun and work well with the veggies.

Olive-Cheese Nuggets make an excellent accompaniment. My friend Myrna made them for a holiday party, and they were such a big hit that everyone was asking for the recipe. (Thank you, Myrna!) For convenience, they can be assembled ahead and refrigerated before being baked and served.

Serves 8

Salad:
 1 lb pasta
 6 oz provolone cheese
 6 oz sharp Maine cheddar cheese
 6 oz havarti with dill cheese
 1 large fresh tomato
 ½ c sun-dried tomatoes packed in oil

Dressing:
 ½ c Raye's Lemon Pepper or Winter
   Garden Mustard*
 ¼ c champagne vinegar
 2 T fresh dill, chopped
 1 t salt
 1 t white pepper
 1 t garlic powder
 ½ c olive oil

Cook the pasta until it is al dente, according to the directions on the package. Drain and set aside. Chill while you prepare the remaining ingredients. Chop the cheeses into ½-inch cubes.

Coarsely chop the fresh tomato. Slice the sun-dried tomatoes into julienne strips.

In a small bowl, combine the mustard, vinegar, dill, salt, pepper, and garlic powder. Slowly whisk in the oil.

In a large bowl, combine the pasta, cheeses, and tomatoes. Pour the dressing over and toss to coat.

Serve chilled on a bed of greens, accompanied by Olive-Cheese Nuggets.

See page 97 for ordering information if this product is not available in your local stores.

Olive-Cheese Nuggets:
  4 oz Maine sharp cheddar cheese, shredded
  4 oz softened butter
  ¾ c flour
  ¼ t salt
  1 t paprika
  24 to 30 medium-size stuffed green olives

Blend shredded cheese and butter. Add dry ingredients. Mix thoroughly.

Scoop a teaspoonful of dough; flatten it in your palm, and place an olive in the center. Form the dough around the olive and pinch the edges together. Repeat with all the olives.

At this point, you can cover and chill for 4 to 5 hours before baking, if you wish.

Place on an ungreased cookie sheet. Bake at 400°F for 12 to 15 minutes, until golden. Serve hot or cold.

If there are any left, store in a sealed container in the refrigerator for up to three days.

DESSERT SALADS

Celebrate the finish of a delectable meal with a small taste of sweet fruit. Here are some of my favorite dessert options.

Warm Harvest Apple Salad with Maple Whipped Cream

Here you have apple pie without the crust. The apples still have that fresh taste, while all the flavors of apple pie melt in your mouth.
Serves 4 to 6

Salad:
2 large Granny Smith apples
2 large Cortland apples
2 large Macintosh apples
1 T lemon juice
1 c golden raisins
½ c calvados or cognac (optional)
2 T pure Maine maple syrup
4 T McIntosh Farm Apple Pie Jam*
½ t cinnamon

Maple Whipped Cream:
1 c heavy cream
1 t vanilla
2 T pure Maine maple syrup

Wash and core the apples. Coarsely chop or slice and toss with the lemon juice.

In a small bowl, place the raisins and calvados (or water, if you choose) to plump.

In a medium saucepan over low heat, whisk the maple syrup, apple pie jam, and cinnamon until the jam is completely dissolved. Add the apples. Taste and adjust sweetness to your liking. Add the raisins and soaking liquid. Heat until the entire mixture is warmed.

In the bowl of an electric mixer pour the cream, vanilla, and maple syrup. Whip the cream until stiff peaks form.

Serve the warm apple salad in a dessert bowl with a dollop of the maple whipped cream on top.

See page 96 for ordering information if this product is not available in your local stores.

Six-Berry Salad with Grand Marnier Zabaglione

Zabaglione is a traditional Italian dessert. Delicious all by itself, this foamy custard is even better spooned over fresh fruit or served with crunchy biscotti. Be sure to have anything else you plan to serve with the zabaglione ready to go, as it really is best eaten just seconds off the stove.
Serves 6

Salad:
  1 pint fresh strawberries
  1 pint fresh raspberries
  1 pint fresh blackberries
  1 pint fresh golden raspberries
  1 pint fresh wild Maine blueberries
  1 pint fresh black raspberries
  2 T Grand Marnier or Warre's Otima Port
  ½ c sifted powdered sugar

Zabaglione:
  6 large egg yolks
  ½ cup sugar
  ¼ c heavy cream
  4 T Grand Marnier or Warre's Otima Port

Wash all of the fruit, saving out 6 delicate strawberries. Hull the remaining strawberries and quarter them. Place all in a large pretty bowl. Toss with the liqueur and the powdered sugar. Chill while you prepare the custard.

In a metal bowl with a whisk or a handheld electric mixer, beat together egg yolks, sugar, and heavy cream. Add liqueur and whisk until combined. Set bowl over a saucepan of barely simmering water, being sure that the water does *not* touch the bottom of the bowl. Beat mixture constantly until tripled in volume—about 5 to 6 minutes. To ensure that the eggs are cooked, beat mixture 3 minutes more.

Spoon the fruit evenly into six decorative bowls and top each serving with a generous dollop of the zabaglione. Garnish each with a whole strawberry, and serve immediately.

Tropical Fruit with Pineapple Dressing
Served with Joe Froggers

We are fortunate to find so many tropical fruits in our local markets. Utilize whatever flavors you like in this tropical dish. It is nice to have a mango, a papaya, and a coconut . . . but the rest is up to you. This dessert is marvelous when served with Joe Froggers (a traditional molasses cookie from my mother's repertoire; see recipe at right). This cookie originated in the 1700s in Marblehead, Massachusetts. Sailors would take the cookies with them when they went to sea. They are delicious when soaked in the juice of the fruit.

Serves 6, with extra cookies

Salad:

1 mango
1 papaya
2 bananas
3 kiwi
1 fresh pineapple (or one 16-oz can of
   pineapple slices)
2 c mandarin oranges
1 c fresh shredded coconut, plus 4 T for garnish
1 c fresh Maine blueberries
3 T fresh lemon juice

Dressing:

4 oz pineapple juice
1 T balsamic vinegar
¼ t salt
1 T grated fresh ginger
3 T pickled ginger, chopped (optional)

Peel and seed the mango and papaya. Chop them coarsely. Peel and slice the bananas, kiwi, and pineapple. Place all in a large bowl. Add the mandarin oranges, coconut, and blueberries. Pour the fresh lemon juice over all ingredients and toss. Chill for 30 minutes.

In a small bowl, whisk together the dressing ingredients. Pour over the fruit and toss. Chill until ready to serve.

To serve, spoon fruit into a pretty bowl or large-mouth wineglass. Rest a Joe Frogger (recipe on next page) beside the fruit and sprinkle with additional coconut.

Joe Froggers:
  1 c shortening or butter
  1 c brown sugar (or 2 c molasses)
  1 c molasses
  1 T fresh grated ginger
  7 c sifted King Arthur all-purpose flour
  2 t salt
  1 t baking powder
  2 t baking soda
  1 t cinnamon
  1 t nutmeg
  1 t cardamom
  ¾ c hot water
  ¼ c rum (optional)

Using an electric mixer, cream the shortening and sugar. Add the molasses and ginger and combine completely. In a separate bowl, sift together the dry ingredients. Mix the hot water and rum. Add the water and dry ingredients alternately to the shortening mixture. The dough will be stiff.

Chill for one hour or up to four days. Roll the dough out on a floured surface to a ¼-inch thickness. Cut into 4-inch circles or strips with a floured glass, cookie cutter, or pizza cutter.

Bake in a preheated 375°F oven for 10 to 12 minutes, or until firm. Remove from oven and cool on rack.

Gingered Pear Salad with Chantilly Cream

This dish is reminiscent of poached pears, but keeps the fresh flavor of the fruit.
Serves 4 to 6

Salad:
  2 ripe Anjou pears
  2 ripe Bosc pears
  2 ripe Asian pears
  1 T lemon juice
  1 T fresh grated ginger
  2 T McIntosh Farm Apple-Ginger Jam*
  ¼ c Warre's Otima or Warrior Ruby Port

Chantilly Cream:
  2 c heavy cream
  1 T vanilla
  1 T McIntosh Farm Apple Ginger Jam*

Pickled ginger for garnish

Wash and core the pears. Coarsely chop or slice and toss with the lemon juice.

In a small bowl, whisk the ginger, apple-ginger jam, and port until the jam is completely dissolved. Pour over the pears and toss. Taste and adjust sweetness to your liking.

In the bowl of an electric mixer, pour the cream, vanilla, and 1 T apple-ginger jam. Whip the cream until stiff peaks form.

Set out 4 pretty plates. Place the pears on each plate. Give each plate of pears a generous dollop of whipped Chantilly cream. Garnish on the side with a little mound of pickled ginger.

* See page 96 for ordering information if this product is not available in your local stores.

DRESSINGS AND MARINADES

VINAIGRETTES —
Why the Proportions Work

Traditional vinaigrette is a combination of oil, vinegar, and flavorings. The simplest method for dressing any salad with these ingredients is to sprinkle your greens with vinegar and drizzle with oil, and then take a nibble and adjust the elements to your taste. Historically, the proportions of vinegar to oil were 1:4. These days we are more fat-conscious, and often enjoy a more acidic dressing with a 1:1 balance. Either way, dressings should be created to best suit both your health and your taste.

The acid element in your dressing can be provided by either vinegar, citrus juice, or a combination of the two. Fruit vinegars and lemon or lime juice create delicate, summery flavors, while cider or red wine vinegar by itself has a slightly more robust taste.

Any combination of vinegar and oil is an emulsion—a mixture where the oil is suspended in tiny droplets within the liquid. Emulsions are considered unstable because they will eventually separate, with the oil coming to the top and the other ingredients sinking to the bottom. Shaking or whisking before your dressing is served easily remedies this. Dressings often include mustard, which helps to blend and hold the ingredients together for a longer time.

Herbs and aromatics are beautiful elements for any dressing. Both fresh and dried herbs add delicate flavor. Aromatics, like chopped onions, shallots, minced garlic, and grated ginger add a new dimension to your salads. These ingredients should all be added to the vinegar along with the salt, and mixed together before the oil is added.

Vinaigrette dressings can also make fine marinades. Your meats will be tender and juicy, with a hint of the flavors of the dressing ingredients.

Dressing made with vinegar may be stored in the refrigerator for up to 3 days. Allow it to sit at room temperature 15 minutes before using. If using lemon juice, make the dressing only 2 hours in advance, as lemon juice tends to lose its freshness. Dressing made with cream (instead of oil) should be used immediately.

Classic Vinaigrette

Makes about ½ cup

1 T red wine vinegar or lemon juice
1 to 2 t Dijon mustard
salt
fresh ground pepper
1 T parsley, finely chopped
1 medium shallot (or scallion), minced
2 T olive oil
2 T canola oil (or 4 T olive oil, or 4 T heavy cream)
1 t finely chopped tarragon (optional)

Food processor method:

Chop the shallots or scallions roughly. Do not mince the parsley or tarragon. Place all ingredients in the blender and pulse 5 to 6 times until blended.

Traditional method:

Pour the vinegar into a shallow soup plate and add the mustard, salt, pepper, parsley, and shallot (as well as tarragon, if using). Mix well with a fork.

Add the oil all at once. Keeping the tines of the fork flat against the bottom of the dish, mix well using a circular motion to emulsify the dressing.

Variations:

For a stronger dressing, ideal for green beans, tomatoes, or cucumbers, use 1½ T of vinegar or lemon juice and 2 t mustard.

For cold vegetable salads with broccoli, asparagus, or leeks, add 1 hard-boiled egg, very finely minced.

Another Classic Vinaigrette

This vinaigrette tastes best with a simple green salad of Boston lettuce, romaine, or green leaf lettuce.
Makes about 1 cup

2 t kosher salt
1 t fresh ground white pepper
½ t fresh ground black pepper
¼ t sugar or Splenda sweetener
½ t dry mustard
1 t Raye's Downeast Schooner Mustard*
2 t lemon juice
2 t garlic, finely chopped
5 T white vinegar
2 T olive oil
10 T vegetable oil

1 raw egg, beaten
½ cup light cream

Place all the ingredients in a 1-pint screw-top jar in the order they are given. Replace top tightly and shake well until the ingredients are completely mixed. Chill before using.

See page 97 for ordering information if this product is not available in your local stores.

Balsamic Vinaigrette

Excellent on fresh baby greens or on a mixed salad of fruit and greens.
Makes about 1¼ cups

1 T olive oil
1 c vegetable oil
2 T red wine vinegar
2 T balsamic vinegar
1½ T light brown sugar
salt and pepper to taste

Place all ingredients in a 1-pint screw-top jar, seal tightly, and shake until the sugar has dissolved.

Roasted Garlic Balsamic Vinaigrette

This dressing is a mild garlic dream. If you like creamy dressings, add ½ c mayonnaise to the finished product; it's delicious either way.
Makes about 1 cup

3 cloves roasted garlic
¼ c balsamic vinegar
⅔ c garlic oil
½ t fresh ground pepper
½ t salt
1 T McIntosh Farm Apple Butter*

Whisk all ingredients together. Serve immediately or chill.

See page 96 for ordering information if this product is not available in your local stores.

Warm Port Vinaigrette

This is an excellent dressing for a salad of greens and sliced pears, sprinkled with Roquefort.
Makes about 3½ cups

3 shallots, minced
2½ c extra virgin olive oil
½ c port
¼ c balsamic vinegar
2½ T honey
2 T fresh lemon juice
salt
fresh ground pepper

Place the shallots in a skillet, pour the oil over them, and heat over medium-high heat until it starts to sizzle. Reduce heat and simmer for 2 minutes; remove from heat.

Whisk port, vinegar, honey, and lemon juice together.

Whisk in the hot shallot and oil mixture, and season with salt and pepper to taste.

It may be used immediately, or stored for later use, covered in the refrigerator. It is best used within a week. When ready to serve, heat the desired amount until it sizzles, and then pour over the salad.

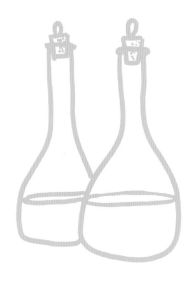

Roquefort Mustard Vinaigrette

This vinaigrette may be used to dress a simple green salad, or used as a dip for a platter of crudités or Buffalo wings. For a real treat, drizzle some on roasted asparagus.
Makes about 2 cups

3 T chicken stock
3 oz crumbled Roquefort
1 egg yolk
1½ T Stonewall Kitchen Champagne
  Shallot Mustard
1 T white wine vinegar
1 t packed brown sugar (light or dark)
¼ c olive oil
1 T chopped chives
salt
fresh ground pepper

Pour the stock into a small bowl and heat in the microwave for about 45 seconds or in a small sauce pan on the top of the stove until warm. Stir the stock and the cheese together to make a smooth paste.

Place the cheese/stock mixture in a blender. Add the egg yolk, mustard, vinegar, and sugar. Blend the ingredients, and with the motor running, add the olive oil in a slow, thin stream.

Pour the mixture into a bowl and stir in the chives. Add salt and pepper to taste. If the mixture is too thick, thin with additional stock.

The dressing may be stored covered in the refrigerator for up to 5 days.

* *See page 97 for ordering information if this product is not available in your local stores.*

Pink Peppercorn Vinaigrette

Serve over poached leeks or grilled spring onions.
Makes about ½ cup

1 T red wine vinegar
2 T fresh lemon juice
3 T olive oil
2 small shallots, very thinly sliced
½ c flat leaf parsley, finely chopped
2 T pink peppercorns, slightly crushed
salt to taste
½ t fresh ground pepper

In a small bowl, whisk the vinegar, lemon juice, and olive oil. Add the shallots, parsley, and pink peppercorns. Season to taste with salt and pepper.

The dressing may be stored covered in the refrigerator for up to 3 days.

Sweet Mustard Horseradish Vinaigrette

Drizzle this dressing over chunked chicken and greens or on cooked Maine shrimp. It is also wonderful as a marinade for steak or buffalo burgers. Check out your local butcher to see what unusual meats are also available.
Makes about ¾ cup

2 t Raye's Brown Ginger Mustard*
2 T distilled white vinegar
½ c olive oil
3 t water
¼ t fresh ground black pepper
1 t fresh horseradish

In a small bowl, whisk all ingredients together. You can store this dressing for up to a week, refrigerated in a covered container.

See page 97 for ordering information if this product is not available in your local stores.

Creamy Avocado Dressing

This is my very own version of green goddess, a mild dressing that works great as a dip, too.
Makes about 2 cups

Makes about 3 cups

2 ripe avocados
2 T garlic, minced
½ c fresh lime juice
2 c mayonnaise (low-fat versions may be used)
1 t sugar or Splenda sweetener
1 t salt
2 t white pepper

Peel, pit, and chunk the avocados, and place them in a food processor. Add the minced garlic and lime juice. Process well until smooth. Add mayonnaise, sugar, salt, and pepper. Process until smooth. Can be thinned with up to 3 T of milk, if necessary.

This is delicious when served with carrot sticks, mushrooms, and scallions, or on a salad of greens and fresh tomatoes. It can be stored in the refrigerator for 4 days. Stir before using.

Oh My Goodness Blue Cheese Dressing

Of course this is wonderful on greens and crunchy garlic croutons, but you can also add a dollop to your favorite hamburger, or serve with roast pork tenderloin and a smidge of applesauce. Or cut a loaf of bread in half horizontally, spread this dressing on liberally, and broil until the top is light brown and bubbling—yum!
Makes about 2½ cups

1½ c mayonnaise
4 T white vinegar
¾ c sour cream
1½ T sugar
¾ t salt
½ t white pepper
¾ c crumbled blue cheese

In a medium glass or stainless-steel bowl, whisk together the mayonnaise, vinegar, sour cream, sugar, salt, and pepper for one minute. Be sure all of the ingredients are well blended and the sugar is dissolved. Gently fold in the blue cheese.

This dressing keeps well for up to a week when stored in an airtight container in the refrigerator.

Parmesan Dill Dressing

Light and refreshing, this dressing will add another layer of creamy flavor to your favorite salad. It's also wonderful on poached salmon on a bed of baby spinach and makes a luscious dip for cooked tortellini (cooled to room temperature).
Makes about 2¾ cups

1½ c sour cream
½ c mayonnaise
3 T chopped fresh parsley
3 T chopped fresh dill
1 t garlic powder (or 1 clove, minced)
1 t Spike powder (seasonings blend)
1 full t fresh ground black pepper
⅔ c fresh grated Parmesan cheese
½ c fresh squeezed lemon juice
zest of 2 lemons

Mix all ingredients together. If you need to thin this dressing, add more lemon juice.

It can be stored up to a week in an airtight container in the refrigerator

Red Chili and Lime Dressing

Take the spice to your limit! Serve chilled on cooked shrimp, chicken, or scallops.
Makes about 2 cups

2 t Tabasco sauce or Asian chili paste
½ c ketchup
1 lime, zested and juiced
2 ribs of celery, finely chopped
1 red bell pepper, seeded and coarsely chopped
1 yellow or orange bell pepper, seeded and
  coarsely chopped
2 to 3 T chopped parsley leaves

salt
fresh ground black pepper

Combine Tabasco (or Asian chili paste), ketchup, lime zest and juice, celery, peppers, and parsley in a small bowl. Add salt and pepper to taste.

Store extra dressing in the refrigerator and use within 3 days.

Summer Herb Dressing

This dressing offers bright flavors that transport you right out to the garden. Use the freshest herbs you can find.
Makes about 2½ cups

2 T Raye's Stone Ground Mustard*
¾ c white vinegar
1 shallot, minced
2 cloves garlic (use roasted garlic here, if you
  have it)
1 T sugar or Splenda sweetener
½ t salt
½ t fresh ground black pepper
¼ c fresh basil, chopped
2 T fresh sage, chopped
2 T fresh thyme, chopped
3 T fresh parsley, chopped
1½ c olive oil

Whisk all of the ingredients but the oil together. Slowly drizzle the oil into the dressing, whisking constantly.

Serve chilled with your choice of greens.

Store extra dressing in the refrigerator and use within 3 days.

See page 97 for ordering information if this product is not available in your local stores.

Sweet Roasted Onion Dressing

This dressing was the biggest hit of our last salad party. McIntosh Farm is located in Madison, Maine, and has the most wonderful jams and jellies. Their apple-pepper jam is delightful in this dressing, or served over cream cheese with crackers.
Makes about 3 cups

1 large Vidalia onion
1 head of garlic
2 c olive oil
2 T McIntosh Farm Apple-Pepper Jam*
4 T cider vinegar
1 t salt
1 t fresh ground black pepper
1 c roasted garlic oil

Cut the ends off of the onion and remove the outer layer of skin. Line a small baking pan with foil, and place the onion in the center of the pan.

Cut the top third off of the head of garlic, exposing the tops of the cloves. Place it in the pan beside the onion. Pour 2 c olive oil over the garlic and onion. Cover with foil. Roast in a 300°F oven for 1 hour. Remove from the oven and let cool.

When cool, hold the bottom of the head of garlic and squeeze the softened cloves out into a small bowl. Measure out 3 T of garlic and place in a measuring cup. Add enough of the roasting oil to make 1 full cup. Set this aside.

(Reserve the remaining oil and garlic for later use. It can be stored in a sealed container in the refrigerator for up to a week. The oil may set up; if so, just let the dressing come to room temperature before using.)

In the bowl of a food processor, place the roasted onion. Process until smooth. Add the apple-pepper jam, cider vinegar, salt, and pepper. Process again until smooth. Slowly drizzle in the cup of roasted garlic oil, processing until thoroughly emulsified.

Store extra dressing in the refrigerator and use within 3 days.

See page 96 for ordering information if this product is not available in your local stores.

Garlic Dressing or Marinade

Use for vegetables to be served raw, grilled, or roasted. It is also wonderful warmed slightly and served with fresh wholegrain bread as a dipping oil.
Makes about ¾ cup

3 cloves garlic, minced
1 lemon, zested and juiced
½ t fresh ground black pepper
1 t sea salt
½ c extra virgin olive oil

Place ingredients in a jar with a tight-fitting lid and shake well.

Store extra dressing in the refrigerator and use within 3 days.

Light Ginger Sesame Dressing or Marinade

This is a great dressing on greens or Asian pasta salads and also makes an excellent marinade for chicken.
Makes about 1½ cups

⅓ c rice or ginger vinegar
½ t garlic, minced
1 shallot, minced
2 T fresh ginger, grated
½ c sesame oil
1 T chili oil
2 T soy sauce
2 T honey
juice of 1 lime

Whisk all ingredients together. Chill until you are ready to use. Whisk again before serving.

Store extra dressing in the refrigerator and use within 3 days.

Lemon Salsa Verde

Serve with veggies for dipping, or on grilled fish or chicken on a bed of greens.
Makes about 7½ cups

3 c tomatillos, chopped
1 c fresh parsley, chopped
2 c Vidalia onions, chopped
1 jalapeño pepper, chopped
1 serrano pepper, chopped
3 cloves of garlic, minced
2 t salt
1 c chives, coarsely chopped
1 c cilantro, coarsely chopped
¼ c white vinegar
1 c fresh lemon juice
1 T sugar or Splenda sweetener
½ c olive oil
⅛ c water (if needed)

Remove dry papery skins from tomatillos and coarsely chop. Place chopped tomatillos in the bowl of a food processor; coarsely purée.

Add parsley, onions, jalapeño, serrano pepper, garlic, salt, chives, and cilantro. Pulse to purée and blend.

Add vinegar, lemon juice, and sugar. Pulse.

Drizzle in the olive oil while the processor is on. Add up to ⅛ c water if necessary to loosen the dressing enough to pour.

Store extra dressing in the refrigerator and use within 3 days.

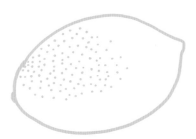

ENHANCEMENTS
The "Wow" Factor

Your choices for salad garnishes are nearly unlimited, ranging from a simple sprinkling of edible flowers, to bits of fruit and vegetable in contrasting colors, to home-made croutons. Toasted nuts and seeds flavored with spices are perfect toppings for many salads. Make your own flavored oils and vinegars to simply sprinkle on salads or use as ingredients in more elaborate dressings. Herb and seasoning blends are also much tastier when made fresh in your own kitchen. You will find recipes for all these salad "enhance-ments" on the following pages.

EDIBLE GARNISHES

There are so many delicious garnishes available in the kitchen garden. The colorful flowers we grow are often a brilliant and peppery addition to any salad. Be sure they are rinsed and free of any pesticides and fertilizer before you consider them edible. It is best to purchase a flora identification handbook to identify *any* plant or flower before you try it. Here are a few suggestions for flowers to use as garnishes:

basil blossoms	garlic blossoms	nasturtium
chamomile	garlic chives	pansy
chive blossoms	hibiscus	rose petals
chrysanthemum	Johnny-jump-ups	squash blossoms
clover	lavender	sunflowers
dandelion	marigold	violets
fuchsia	mint	

Other options for simple and attractive garnishes can be found in the cabinet or refrigerator:

artichoke petals	toasted nuts	roasted red peppers
breadsticks	peapods (fresh)	rosemary
cheeses (hard or semi-hard), shredded	pickled ginger (in a small "haystack")	salsa, sour cream, and avocado slices
chili peppers of all sorts	pickles	sesame sticks
citrus slices	pimentos, sliced	sun-dried tomatoes, sliced
dried fruit	puff pastry sticks	sunflower seeds
fresh herbs, chopped	relish	vegetables, shredded

FLAVORED OILS

Garlic Oil

This oil is fantastic! It is quick and simple. Use it in place of your oil in salad dressing recipes, when sautéing or stir-frying, or to dunk your bread.
Makes 2 cups

16 oz extra virgin olive oil
4 to 6 cloves garlic, minced or pressed
10 peppercorns
1 shallot, minced

Place all the ingredients in a medium saucepan. Heat slowly until oil is hot, but not smoking.

Remove from heat and let oil cool. When cool, strain through a cheesecloth-lined sieve. Pour into a clean jar with a lid and store in the refrigerator. If it begins to solidify, leave it out at room temperature for 30 minutes before you intend to serve. This oil can be stored up to a week.

Serve in a small dish, adding a few grinds of black pepper and a sprinkle of sea salt. Dunk a piece of crusty bread in the oil, and voilà—the perfect accompaniment for any salad!

Lemon-Garlic Oil

Makes 2 cups

3 garlic cloves (peeled)
3 generous lemon wedges
16 oz extra virgin olive oil

Alternate lemon and garlic on a bamboo skewer. Place skewer in a bottle. Fill bottle with oil. Cover or cork tightly.

Allow 1 week for flavors to develop. Will keep in a cool place for two months.

Rosemary Oil

In a pinch you can substitute 4 T dried rosemary, but fresh is best for this recipe. Serve with crusty bread, which is always delicious alongside any salad.
Makes 2 cups

16 oz extra virgin olive oil
4 stalks of fresh rosemary, plus 2 stalks to place
   in the finished bottle
10 chives, minced
5 peppercorns plus 3 to add to the
   finished bottle
2 scallions, sliced in half lengthwise

Place all the ingredients in a medium saucepan. Heat slowly until oil is hot, but not smoking.

Remove from heat and let oil cool. When cool, strain through a cheesecloth-lined sieve.

Place 2 fresh stalks of rosemary and three peppercorns into a clean jar with a lid. Pour the cool oil over the rosemary and peppercorns, and store. Will keep in a cool place for two months.

Serve in a small dish, adding a few slices of fresh chives, a snip of fresh rosemary, a few grinds of black pepper, and a sprinkle of sea salt.

Raspberry or Blueberry Vinegar

Fruit vinegars used to be a staple of fancy restaurants. Now you can make your own fresh version using your favorite fruits. You can also try the recipe below with peaches, pears, or other fruit available to you.
Makes 1 cup

1 c Maine raspberries or blueberries
1 c white vinegar

Place both ingredients in a glass bottle. Shake. Keep bottle in a cool place and shake daily for 1 week.

Strain liquid through a fine mesh strainer or cheesecloth to remove all solids. Pour your fruit vinegar into a clean glass bottle. Store in the refrigerator for up to 3 months.

Quick version: Mix equal parts of fruit juice and white vinegar. Allow mixture to sit overnight before you use it. This also will keep well for up to three months.

Ginger Vinegar

Makes 1 cup

1 c white vinegar
1 large chunk (about 1 oz) ginger

Place vinegar in a clean glass jar with a lid. Wash and coarsely chop the ginger and add to the vinegar. Cover.

Let mixture sit in the refrigerator for three days before using. You can add more vinegar and more ginger as you use the flavored vinegar, to keep enough on hand. Store in the refrigerator for up to three months.

Herb Mixture for Dressing or Cheese

It's convenient to have this herb mixture on hand for tossing into salad dressing, blending into cream cheese or chèvre, or just sprinkling on fresh veggies. The following proportions work very well with either fresh or dried herbs.
Makes a scant 1½ cup

3 T oregano
6 T dill weed
3 T marjoram
3 T thyme
3 T basil
1 t garlic powder
2 t white pepper
3 T parsley

Mix all herbs together in a bowl. Use in your favorite salad dressing recipe, replacing an equal amount of the herbs in the original ingredients list.

For herbed cheese, add 2 T of the mixture to 8 oz of cream cheese or chèvre, and incorporate completely.

Curry Seasoning Blend

This is delicious on chicken salad, sprinkled in basic dressing, or used to spice up seeds and nuts. The fenugreek seeds can be found in your grocery's spice aisle or at an Asian specialty store.
Makes about ¾ cup

1 T turmeric
1 T cumin
1 t red pepper flakes
1 t onion powder
1 t ginger
1 t garlic powder
1 T sugar or Splenda sweetener
1 T salt
1 t white pepper
1 t coriander
1 T fenugreek seeds
¼ t cloves
1 t dry mustard

Mix all ingredients together in a small bowl. Store in a small jar with a lid.

You can keep this mixture for up to two months before the flavors start to fade.

Fines Herbes

This blend gives a provençal flavor to any dish. It is used in the Tarragon Cucumber Pasta Salad recipe found in the "Side Salads" chapter.
Makes ½ cup fresh or ¼ cup dried

2 T fresh parsley, chopped (or 1 T dried)
2 T fresh tarragon, chopped (or 1 T dried)
2 T fresh chervil, chopped (or 1 T dried)
2 T fresh chives, chopped (or 1 T dried)

Mix all ingredients together in a small bowl.

If you use fresh herbs, this mixture should be used right away. If you use dried herbs, you can store them in a sealed jar for up to two months.

Seasoned Salt Substitute

For those of us watching our sodium intake, here is a flavorful solution.
Makes about 8 tablespoons

1 T white or black pepper
2 T dried savory
1 t to 1 T crushed red pepper (to your taste)
1 T onion powder
2 T dried parsley
1 T garlic powder
2 t citric acid
1 T dried lemon peel

Mix all ingredients together in a small bowl. Store in a small jar with a lid.

You can keep this mixture for up to two months before the flavors start to fade.

Aromatic Macadamias

2½ c macadamia nuts
2 T oil
1½ t cumin
½ t cayenne
2 T sugar
1 t salt

Preheat the oven to 300°F. Pour the oil in a small pan, and heat until warm. Add cumin, cayenne, sugar, and salt, stirring until aromatic. Pour spiced oil over the nuts and toss to coat evenly.

Spread nuts out on a cookie sheet in a single layer. Bake for 20 minutes, stirring them every five minutes. When they are done, cool until easy to handle and sprinkle on your favorite salad.

Stored in an airtight container, these will keep for a week.

Sweet Cinnamon Walnuts

1 c sugar
½ c cold water
¾ t salt
1 t pure vanilla
1 t cinnamon
4 c walnuts

Place the sugar, water, and salt in a saucepan. Stir and bring to a boil, until the mixture reaches 240°F on a candy thermometer (about 4 minutes).

Add the vanilla and cinnamon. Stir until blended. The mixture may bubble up and splatter, so be careful.

Add the nuts. Stir to coat evenly, and immediately pour out onto a cookie sheet lined with parchment or waxed paper. Cool until easy to handle. If necessary, break nuts apart before serving. Serve on top of or as an accompaniment to your favorite salad.

Stored in an airtight container, these will keep for a week.

Spiced Toasted Pecans

1 lb shelled pecans
1 t salt
1 t crushed red pepper flakes
1 t garlic powder
2 T olive oil

Place the pecans on a parchment- or silicone-lined baking sheet. Preheat the oven to 275°F.

In a small bowl, mix together the salt, red pepper flakes, garlic powder, and olive oil. Pour oil mixture over the nuts and toss to coat evenly.

Bake for 10 minutes; stir, and bake for 10 more minutes. Cool until easy to handle and sprinkle on your favorite salad.

Stored in an airtight container in the refrigerator, these will keep for a week.

Crunch Topping

This is a delicious alternative to croutons. Feel free to add seeds and nuts.

2 c oats
⅓ c wheat germ
½ c melted butter
¼ t onion salt
¼ t garlic powder
⅓ c grated Parmesan cheese

In a small bowl, combine all the ingredients. Mix well.

Bake in a preheated 275°F oven for 15 to 18 minutes. Stir every three minutes. When crunch topping is cooked, let cool 20 minutes before sprinkling on salad.

Store in an airtight container in the refrigerator for up to a week.

Seed Topping

This is a great topping to sprinkle generously over salads for extra crunch and fiber.

3 T butter
½ t salt
⅛ t cayenne pepper
1 T soy sauce (or Worcestershire sauce)
¼ c oatmeal
¼ c poppy seeds
¼ c sesame seeds
¼ c flax seeds
1 T olive oil or butter or baking spray
  for greasing the pan

Melt the butter in the microwave or in a small saucepan over low heat. Add the salt, pepper, and soy sauce (or Worcestershire sauce). Stir well.

In a medium bowl, place the oatmeal, poppy seeds, sesame seeds, and flax seeds. Stir well. Pour the liquid ingredients over the seeds and stir to coat evenly.

Line a baking sheet with parchment or foil. Spray lightly with baking spray. Pour out the seeds and shake gently to form a single thin layer.

Bake at 275°F for 15 minutes. Check them every five minutes, and remove the pan when they smell aromatic and are lightly golden brown.

Spoon mixture into a bowl and cool until you are ready to use. Can be stored tightly covered in a cool, dry place for up to two weeks.

Rosemary Foccacia Croutons

Foccacia is a thin, herb-infused bread that is often served alongside a salad. This recipe is quick and easy. It can be served in wedges or slices, or cut into cubes for croutons, which are great sprinkled on the Baby Spinach Salad with Rosemary Chèvre and Blueberry Vinaigrette (p. 33).

1 c warm water or potato water (water used to boil your potatoes)
1 t brown sugar
1½ T yeast

3 to 4 c King Arthur all-purpose flour
1 t garlic powder
1 t chopped parsley
1 t onion powder
1 T salt
2 T chopped fresh rosemary
3 T vegetable oil

3 T olive oil
2 T chopped rosemary
4 T fresh grated Parmesan cheese
1 t sea salt
black pepper to taste

In a small bowl, mix the water, brown sugar, and yeast; let sit 5 minutes for the yeast to proof.

In a large bowl, place 3 c flour, garlic powder, parsley, onion powder, salt, and rosemary.

When the yeast is frothy, pour into the dry ingredients and mix. Add the 3 T vegetable oil. Blend the ingredients well. When the mixture begins to form a ball, turn it out onto a floured surface. Knead for 5 minutes. Cover and let the dough rise for 15 minutes.

Gently stretch out the dough. You can use two cookie sheets for thinner foccacia, or one for a thicker loaf. Pull the dough to fit the pan. Press it down with the tips of your fingers to make indentations. The dough should be covered with dimples.

Drizzle the dough with the 3 T olive oil. Spread it around with your palms. Sprinkle the rosemary, Parmesan, sea salt, and pepper on top.

Bake in a preheated 475°F oven for 20 minutes, or until baked through and lightly golden. Place baked foccacia on a rack to cool.

To make the croutons:

4 t butter, melted*
1 t garlic powder*
1 t salt
1 t black pepper
1 t dried rosemary (or 1 T fresh)

Preheat oven to 275°F.

Cut the cooled focaccia into half-inch cubes and place in a large bowl or a large resealable plastic bag. Drizzle the melted butter or oil over the cubes and sprinkle on the seasonings. Toss well to coat evenly.

Spread the cubes on a baking sheet and toast in the oven for 20 minutes.

Store the cooled croutons in a resealable bag (you can use the same one as before). These will keep well for up to a week, or even longer when frozen. To crisp up frozen croutons, toast them for 10 minutes in a 275°F oven.

Or use garlic oil in place of the melted butter and garlic powder.

Garlic Croutons

This is a great way to use day-old baguettes or any crusty bread. You can even cube your bread and place it in a sealed container in the freezer, to use later when you are ready to make the croutons.

1 loaf of day-old French bread, baguette,
   or any crusty bread
4 oz butter
2 cloves garlic, minced
½ t salt
½ t white pepper
1 T chopped fresh or dried parsley
1 T chopped fresh or dried rosemary

Cube the bread to the size you prefer (I like a ½ - to ¾-inch cube). Place on a rack over a cookie sheet and bake in a 300°F oven for 8 minutes, or until completely dry.

Melt the butter in a microwave-safe dish or in a small saucepan. Add remaining ingredients to the butter and stir well.

Pour the crisp bread cubes into a large plastic resealable bag. Pour the butter mixture over the bread in the bag. Seal the bag and shake to coat all of the bread cubes evenly.

Place the seasoned bread cubes back on the rack over the cookie sheet and bake an additional 10 minutes. Let cool on rack and store in a sealed container until you are ready to use. The flavor is best if used within a day or two, but if frozen in a sealed bag or container, they will last four months.

APPENDIXES

Specialty Products from Maine Producers

These excellent products are listed in the ingredients for many recipes in *Fresh Maine Salads*. Most of the addresses and descriptions below come from the Get Real Maine website: www.getreal-maine.com.

Clark Farms

Jigger Clark
Upper Main Street
Damariscotta, ME 04543
Phone: (207) 563-6866

"Wonderful fresh fruit and vegetables, homemade desserts and lobsters cooked to order."

Laughing Stock Farm

Lisa Turner
79 Wardtown Road
Freeport, ME 04032
Phone: (207) 865-3743
E-mail: lisa@laughingstockfarm.com

Laughing Stock Farm grows fresh certified organic vegetables for Portland's finest restaurants and natural food stores. Greens and root crops are grown all winter long in greenhouses heated by burning used cooking oil from local restaurants.

Maine Munchies

P.O. Box 970
Bar Harbor, ME 04609
Phone: (207) 669-6046
Toll-free: (866) 480-0000
Website: www.mainemunchies.com

Dried wild Maine blueberries.

McIntosh Farm Apple Products

Jennifer Dimock
97 Orchard Road
Madison, ME 04950
Phone: (207) 696-5109
Toll-free: (877) 696-5109
E-mail: northstarorchards@tds.net

"Specialty apple products made in our farm kitchen using our own McIntosh apples. Our line includes apple butter, apple syrup, and a variety of apple jams and jellies."

Mystique Cheese

Marje Lupien
P.O. Box 254
Waldoboro, ME 04572
Phone: (207) 832-5136

"Mystique Cheese has been producing chèvre (goat cheese) since 1970, giving the business the distinction of being the oldest producer in the state. They sell a variety of soft cheeses: plain, herb and garlic, roasted garlic, orange, Kahlúa, and chèvre."

Oyster Creek Farm Mushroom Company

Candice and Dan Heydon
61 Standpipe Road
Damariscotta, ME 04543-9715
Phone: (207) 563-1076
Fax: (207) 563-1076
E-mail: mushroom@lincoln.midcoast.com
Website: http://www.oystercreekmushroom.com

"We offer a full line of wild gourmet mushrooms, dried in individual serving sizes, as well as bulk for restaurants. Mushroom powders, oils, and gift boxes are also available."

Raye's Mustard Mill

Nancy Raye
P.O. Box 2
Eastport, ME 04631
Phone: (207) 853-4451
Toll-free: (800) 853-1903
Fax: (207) 853-2937
E-mail: mustards@rayesmustard.com
Website: http://www.rayesmustard.com

"We manufacture more than a dozen varieties of 100% stone-ground mustard in a century-old mill. They are ground and aged by the method used for 500 years, resulting in uniquely piquant and full-bodied flavor."

Simpson's Ocean Fresh Seafood

690 Bath Road
Wiscasset, ME 04578
Phone: (207) 882-9667 or (800) 882-9667

"The freshest seafood in Maine. Delicious Maine lobsters, fish, and shrimp available daily. Sushi grade and smoked seafoods available."

State of Maine Cheese Co., LLC

Cathe Morrill
461 Commercial Street
Rockport, ME 04856
Phone: (207) 236-8895
Toll-free: (800) 762-8895
Fax: (207) 236-9591
E-mail: info@cheese-me.com
Website: http://www.cheese-me.com

"Our factory store showcases our all-natural mild and sharp cheddars, plain and spiced Monterey Jack cheeses, and occasionally certified organic cheeses. Packaged in sizes from random-sized bricks and wedges to 40-pound blocks."

Stonewall Kitchen

Stonewall Lane
York, ME 03909
Phone: (207) 351-2712 or (800) 207-5267
E-mail: guestservices@stonewallkitchen.com
Website: http://www.StonewallKitchen.com

"Our nationally recognized specialty foods are a testament to the art of preserve making and the growing public interest in wholesome, healthy, and tasty ingredients. They are true tributes to our native New England agriculture."

Wolfe's Neck Farm

184 Burnett Road
Freeport, ME 04032
Phone:(207) 865-4469
Fax: (207) 865-6927
E-mail: farmaine@wolfesneckfarm.org
Website: http://www.wolfesneckfarm.org

Wolfe's Neck Farm is a supplier of Certified Organic beef to many large grocery chains. Their meats are healthy and free from chemicals.

Wyman's Blueberry Products

Ann Davis
PO Box 100
Milbridge, ME 04568
Phone: (800) 341-1758
Fax: (207) 546-2074
E-mail: ann@wymans.com
Website: http://www.wymans.com

Wyman's offers a line of frozen berries, canned berries, and juice. If you are unable to find what you need at your local retailer, you can contact Wyman's for direct shipping. Their one-case-minimum orders for frozen fruit must be shipped overnight.

Complement Your Fresh Salad with Fresh Bread

The best baking products anywhere come from the King Arthur Flour Company in nearby Vermont. Their flours are consistently excellent. Most Maine groceries carry King Arthur's basic all-purpose and bread flours, but the company offers other specialty flours and many other items at their retail store and through their catalogue and website.

King Arthur Flour
The Baker's Catalogue
58 Billings Farm Road
White River Junction, VT 05001
Phone: (800) 827-6836
Web: www.kingarthurflour.com

Farmers' Markets in Maine

Farmers' markets are located throughout the state, and each offers a unique blend of personalities and products. The exact times and locations can vary from one year to the next, so I will not attempt to include a comprehensive list in these pages. *The Maine Farmers' Markets* booklet, published by the Maine Department of Agriculture, "will help you find delicious foods and high-quality agricultural products—fruits and vegetables, flowers and plants, meats and cheeses, breads and bakery products, eggs, crafts, and specialty foods—produced locally, harvested fresh, and sold directly to you by the farmers, your neighbors." The booklet offers a map with listings by product and location.

You can find the freshest foods at these markets, not to mention unusual and heirloom varieties. Your meals and your community will both benefit. The authors of the *Maine Farmers' Markets* booklet sum it up well: "Your support of local farms strengthens the local economy, protects our rural landscape, and provides you and your family a reliable source of local, fresh food."

So, check local papers for information, get a copy of *Maine Farmers' Markets,* or check the Department of Agriculture's www.getrealmaine.com website.

Grow Your Own Fresh Ingredients

Moose Crossing Garden Center
Ben Lupien
US Route One
Waldoboro, ME
Phone: (207) 832-4282   Fax: (207) 832-4282
E-mail: t_lupine@hotmail.com

"Fresh herbs, seeds, perennials, annuals, and vegetable plants for your patio and garden."

Preserving Our
Maine Farms

The family farm is one of the most recognizable icons of America's cultural heritage. With more than 7,213 farms, Maine has the greatest number of farms of any state in New England. Maine's agricultural producers and processors add more than 1.2 billion dollars to Maine's economy every year. Agriculture is a powerful business sector, which embodies Maine's entrepreneurial spirit at every scale. As much as Maine farms may vary in personality and purpose, they all share something essential because they embody values derived from working the land, values that touch all sorts of different people. Preserving Maine's farms and farmland means sustaining a complex web of relationships that connects farmers to people in every aspect of life in Maine.

Adapted from the brochure *Preserving Our Farms and Farmland,* published by the Maine Farmland Protection Program, Maine Department of Agriculture.

For More Information about Maine Foods

Maine Alternative Poultry Association
Gary Balducci: (207) 882-5407
Ruth Robinson: eggladie@aol.com

Maine Dairy Promotion Board/Maine Dairy & Nutrition Council
Phone: (207) 287-3621
www.drinkmainemilk.org

Maine Deer and Elk Farmers Association
www.mdefa.com

Maine Department of Agriculture Market and Production Development
Phone: (207) 287-3491
www.getrealmaine.com

An invaluable source for locating everything you might need.

Maine Department of Marine Resources
Phone: (207) 624-6550
www.maineseafood.org

Maine Farm Vacation Bed & Breakfast Association
www.mainefarmvacation.com

Maine Lobster Promotion Council
Phone: (207) 947-2966
www.mainelobsterpromo.com

Maine Maple Producers Association
Phone: (207) 474-5262
www.mainemapleproducers.com

Maine Organic Farmers & Gardeners Association (MOFGA)
Phone: (207) 568-4142
www.mofga.org

Maine Pomological Society
www.maineapples.org

Maine Potato Board
Phone: (207) 769-5061
www.mainepotatoes.com

Maine Sheep Breeders Association
www.mainesheepbreeders.org

Wild Blueberry Association of North America
Phone: (207) 288-2655
www.wildblueberries.com

Note: Metric measures have been rounded to the nearest whole unit for ease of use.

VOLUME

U.S. measures	Metric (Milliliters)
⅛ t	0.5
¼ t	1
½ t	2
1 t	5
½ T	7
1 T (3 teaspoons)	15
2 T (1 fluid ounce)	30
¼ c (4 tablespoons)	60
⅓ c	80
½ c (4 fluid ounces)	125
⅔ c	160
¾ c (6 fluid ounces)	180
1 c (16 tablespoons)	250
1 pt (2 cups)	500 (scant)
1 qt (4 cups)	1 liter (scant)

DIMENSIONS

U.S. (Inches)	Metric (Centimeters)
⅛	0.3
¼	0.6
½	1.3
¾	1.9
1	2.5

WEIGHT

U.S. (Ounces, pounds)	Metric (Grams)
½	15
1	30
2	60
3	85
¼ lb (4 oz)	115
½ lb (8 oz)	225
¾ lb (12 oz)	340
1 lb (16 oz)	450

TEMPERATURE

Degrees Fahrenheit	Degrees Celsius
250	130
275	140
300	150
325	160
350	180
375	190
400	200
425	220
450	230
475	246
500	250

INDEX

Index

Also from Down East Books

Far East / Down East
Maine's Freshest Foods Spiced with Asia's Finest Flavors

Bruce deMustchine

"Recipes for adventurous tastes. . . . Maine seafood works wonderfully with Asian preparations and ingredients." —*Down East* magazine

Hardcover, 112 pages, 73 color photos, 8¾" x 10¼" $28.00

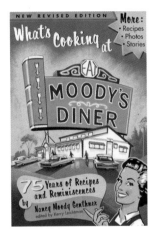

What's Cooking at Moody's Diner
75 Years of Recipes and Reminiscences

Nancy Moody Genthner

"This humble diner has reached a status approaching that of a national icon."
—*Newsday*, Long Island, New York

Paperback, 208 pages, 91 b&w photos, 6" x 9" $12.95

The Maine Sporting Camp Cookbook
More Than 400 Favorite Recipes

Alice Arlen

"One of the most intriguing cookbooks to have crossed my desk in a long time."
—*Shooting Sportsman* magazine

Paperback, 272 pages, 7" x 9½" $18.95

Available wherever books are sold or directly from Down East Books
www.downeastbooks.com • 800-685-7962